MW00907211

EXODUS:
OUR STORY TOO!

From Slavery to the World to

the Kingdom of God

PATRICIA SAID ADAMS

ISBN- 13: 978-1974610914
ISBN- 10: 1974610918

Editing/Interior Book Design & Cover Layout:
CBM Christian Book Editing
www.christian-book-editing.com

Printed in the United States of America

TABLE OF CONTENTS

Foreword

It is hard to know where to begin to acknowledge all the influences in my life who have helped me to write this book. First of all, I have to say that the Holy Spirit who has directed my life in all ways for over thirty years, who has put up with all my wrestling for control and my limited thinking about myself for all those years—He has brought me to the place where I could write this book. He inspired the idea in the first place. He has, over the years, taught me what I needed to know. He has directed me through a number of "training" programs from actual courses to lessons learned from the normal pain and challenges of my life in order to bring me to where I could begin to love. He has done for me what He has done for anyone who would place themselves in His hands. I am eternally grateful for the life He has given me.

Aside from raising my wonderful children, Jennifer, Peter and Jonathan, who taught me more about life and love just by being who they are, it was my spiritual direction training at the Spiritual Direction Institute at the Mercy Center in Burlingame, CA, which changed everything about me. To learn how to be present to another, to the Holy Spirit and myself in a session, giving up my own desires for the directee, and following the Spirit's lead, taught me so much about putting God and the other first. To sit with many directees and feel the great privilege to attend to their deepest desires transformed me. My two spiritual directors, Rita Kaufman (10 years) and Kathleen Moloney-Tarr (7 years), have given me the space and permission to be myself in God.

I count on two groups here in Charlotte for honest sharing about where we are and spiritual support for the journey. Our GALS group which began in deep gratitude and continues to nourish us—Pattie Butler, Heather Brody, Joan Hope, Jinny Sullivan and Gretchen Woolsey. And my band in the Wesleyan Contemplative (Lay) Order is rooted in Centering Prayer and deep sharing—Teri and Roger Strom, Anne Hilborn, Becky Owen, Trish Pegram and Johanna Miller. I give all of them my thanks for their support along the way.

And many thanks go to the many readers of my blog on Facebook, *By the Waters,* who have contributed their own stories to illustrate what I am trying to say. They are unnamed to protect their privacy, but hopefully will recognize themselves in the book. My apologies to those whose stories I didn't use. My choice had nothing to do with the value of or any judgment about your story, but only about what needed to be said in each section. My readers' comments on Facebook, inspire so much in my writing and in my life.

And finally, my gratitude to all the folks at CBM Christian Book Marketing who edited and worked to promote my book and to give it a place in the publishing world today.

Introduction

The Exodus story is the great epic of the Old Testament. It takes five books of the Bible to tell the tale. It's not just the story of the Israelites and how God led them out of slavery in Egypt and, finally, settled them in Canaan. As with many other stories in the Bible, it is a story for everyone who loves God and who would love to be able to bring their whole selves to God. It is the great template that God has left us for how we go from slavery to the world's ways to God's ways, to living in the Kingdom of God.

The story follows the traditional, classic spiritual journey in its steps of *awakening, purgation, illumination and union.*[1] We will be looking at the Exodus story through the lens of these steps. The longest part of the journey is the wilderness experience, a place where no one wishes to stay. Its barrenness, however, facilitates God's desire to reshape those who would love Him and follow Him wherever He would take them. After the years spent in the wilderness, the Israelites have been transformed into people who can live in His Kingdom, obeying God's will, expressing His qualities of peace, love, and goodness.

It's easy for us to see that the Israelites were enslaved—they are foreigners in Egypt; there were Egyptian masters who beat them if they didn't make their quotas of bricks. As the story about God leading the Israelites out of Egypt begins, they've just had their workloads doubled. The Pharaoh is an autocrat who uses them to sustain and grow

[1] Benedict J. Groeschel, *Spiritual Passages: The Psychology of Spiritual Development*, Crossroad Publishing Company, New York, Chapter 4, p. 66-87

his wealth and power, enslaving them to keep them from rebelling. They have no freedom.

But slavery to the Egyptians was a surprise to the Israelites. They had come—all eleven brothers (sons of Jacob) and their families—when there was a famine in their land. Well, you probably know the story: Joseph's brothers had sold him into slavery and he had been brought to Egypt, where he had eventually prospered as an advisor to the Pharaoh. And when the famine came, his brothers came seeking grain to keep them alive and they found Joseph in charge. Then, at his invitation, all the descendants of Jacob, and Jacob himself, moved to this new land. They did so well there that they became a threat to a new Pharaoh who oppressed them and put slave masters over them. They had to work making bricks and in the fields.

Then there is the story of Moses as a baby that we all know well, too. The Pharaoh had told the Hebrew midwives to kill all the Israelite boys born and to let the girl babies live. When a Levite woman gave birth to a son, she hid him in a basket and put him in the Nile near where the Pharaoh's daughter was bathing. Upon discovering the baby in the reeds, the Pharaoh's daughter hired the mother to wet-nurse him until he was weaned. Then, he was raised as a child of the Pharaoh's daughter.

Our own slavery to the world's ways is not so easy for us to discern. First, we've grown up in the system that enslaves us. Second, we've adopted the world's thinking about ourselves as very young children, capitulated to the self-images the world offers us, not knowing that by looking deeper into ourselves beyond what the culture taught us, we would find another way to live. A way that is congruent, integral to who we were created to be by God.

So, we buy into the kind of oppression that seems normal and convinces us that it is the only way to be. Each culture has its own version of the world's viewpoint, but mainly we humans are so self-protective of ourselves and of our own people that anyone who is different from us is perceived as a threat. We are so self-involved, so culturally-involved, that we can only see life as we imagine it to be, using our own limited point of view. And we are so fearful of any pain and suffering that we find many ways of pushing the pain of slavery away—watching TV, playing endless video games, drinking, taking drugs, always having our nose in a book, always going shopping and spending money, always checking our phones--and many other options which become addictive.

Everything we see happening around us, we view through our cultures' and our own personal lenses. Even religious teachings, which would open up how we feel about other peoples and about God, are skewed, so that they fit the cultural paradigm. And so, we miss God's invitation to something much more than we know. We may not lead deeply satisfying lives, but all other roads are closed to us because of the limitations of our personal and cultural lenses.

Into this very restricted way of seeing the world and its possibilities for us come the Biblical teachings about the Exodus story. As I have read and studied it over the last four years, I have become convinced that it is the "template" that God has left us for how we can move from slavery to the world to the freedom to be who we were created to be by

God. The goal is for us to live in God's Kingdom where love and forgiveness, purpose and fulfillment for us reign here on Earth. We might also describe this movement as going from the false self to the true self, from fear to faith, from proud to humble, from ego-centered to soul-centered, from a me-centered perspective, to a God-centered perspective.

So, God calls us out of slavery to a whole new kind of freedom. To live in God's Kingdom often just sounds like another kind of slavery to us: being obedient to His laws, every dot and tittle, putting Him first in our lives, but the experience of being obedient to God and in a close relationship with Him brings a kind of freedom we have never before tasted. Interestingly, the Hebrew word for obedience, shama,[2] means to hear, to listen and to obey. It is the freedom of being inner-referenced, rather than outer-referenced. We no longer have to worry about what anyone else thinks of what we are doing. We only care about the judgment of our souls, which is where the Indwelling Spirit of God dwells. In our souls lies the potential to be all that we were created to be, to use our gifts and talents and even challenges in our own unique way. It means that our burdens are shared, not shouldered alone.[3] Obedience to God feels like freedom! Amazing! It's not another kind of bondage? No!

God is calling us out of slavery, just as He called the Israelites out of Egypt. In this book, we will be exploring what the story of Exodus has to tell us about our own story

---

[2] http://www.abarim-publications.com/Meaning/Shama.html#.WEIz_6IrLVo 12/8/16
[3] Matthew 11:30 Jesus says, "For my yoke is easy and my burden light."

and where God would take us when He leads us out of our own "Egypt." We will follow the trajectory of the Israelites from Moses, dealing with Pharaoh, to Joshua leading them into the Promised Land - after forty years of wandering in the wilderness. We'll be looking at what happens to us in the wilderness and why that long time there is necessary. We'll see the huge part that rebellion plays in our human story. And we'll be looking at the kind of challenges we will face in the Promised Land, just as the Israelites did. We will be exploring the classic four steps in a spiritual journey.

Awakening

Awakening is the first step of acknowledging God's call in our lives to a fuller life, a life lived abundantly. Longing for more to life than slavery, we are called out of a state of dissatisfaction with the way things are. We are called to a more integrated life, a life lived beneath the surface busyness and turmoil. A favorite metaphor of mine is of the ocean. All the surface activity takes place in the top fifteen feet or so of the ocean—that is, the waves, the choppiness, the white caps, the raging water of storms. Beneath the surface are long, slow currents that seemingly go on forever.

Only a Tsunami shakes those deeper waters. And so it is with our lives: all the surface activity fails to touch the deeper currents of our lives: the deeper, truer self, the soul. And it is in the soul that we are deeply connected to God. The soul holds the created agenda for our lives. It is the part of us that "hears" the "still, small voice" of God,[4] the part of

---

[4] 1 Kings 19:12 KJV

us that was created in God's own image. [5]It is where the Indwelling Spirit of God dwells.

Until we begin to pay attention to that "gentle whisper"[6] the potential relationship with God lies dormant within us. As we start to pay attention, it becomes more and more active. We depend on its leadership more and more. And so, the Holy Spirit's influence within us grows into a partnership in which we participate with God in the created agenda for our lives, our own unique way of bringing in the Kingdom of God using our gifts and talents plus what we have learned from our suffering and pain. We are to express through these gifts the love that defines God, to be "the light of the world,"[7] and a demonstration of a life lived in the Kingdom. Gradually, we experience the diminishing influence of our ego and the growing importance of God in our lives and our serving Him through helping others in our own unique way.

Another way of expressing this change in the way we are, in how we do everything we do is this: We are to be converted from the world's ways of thinking and being, into God's ways. Our awakening to God's call may come from a dissatisfaction with the way things are in our lives, a kind of unfulfilled hell or undefined longing. Or it may be a disaster, which flings us out of "Egypt" and lands us in the wilderness. Many people experienced extreme life changes as Hurricane Katrina in 2005 ravaged the New Orleans area; they had to move away immediately or perish. It might be

---

[5] Genesis 1:27
[6] 1 Kings 19:12
[7] Matthew 5:14

an illness or the premature death of a love one that lands us in the unknown territory of the wilderness.

It is not easy to leave the familiar, even if it is toxic to us. We depend on the environment in which we live to define us, set our context, be our home base. It's not easy to change the very basis of our lives, to live in a new place where we have to start over again. We can be lead out of Egypt, if we are willing, or just wake up to find ourselves in a totally changed world.

Purgation

Whether we have been led out of "Egypt", or we find ourselves extricated somewhat violently from the place of slavery, we are more and more willing to listen to God's voice within, more and more dependent on Him to help us in the extremes of the wilderness in which we find ourselves. We need His guidance and leading; this new and barren place is frightening to us. We depend on His providence for food, drink and all our needs. This first part of the wilderness story through Mount Sinai is the first stage of *purgation*, a cleansing of our dependence on the ways of the world. It is essential to be purged of these ways, so that we can conform to God's ways, if we are to enter the Kingdom eventually.

We find ourselves in limbo in the wilderness, neither in "Egypt" nor in the Promised Land. This is a time a real anxiety, because we are only starting out with God and we don't have any idea of how we're going to survive. In this first part of the wilderness sojourn, we are to cease the obvious sins and our willful disobedience in order to follow where He would lead us. This is the *purgation* of what gets in between us and God, at least the obvious barriers. This call for obedience may feel like we have to rigidly adhere to the laws and to God's ways, but it is more about aligning ourselves with His desires. In other words, it is not about a rigid control of what we do and how we do it. It is more about our desire to please God.

In the second part of the wilderness after Mount Sinai *purgation* will continue in us digging into deeper and deeper levels of the self, more at the level of our attitudes and our pain and suffering. We are to be purged of all in us that rebels against God, that keeps us self-centered, that acts out of our personal and cultural lenses.

The closer we draw to God, the more we bring our whole selves to God in love, the more we are able to conform to what He wants for us. We would not want to violate any of His boundaries when we love Him. And it's this purging that enables us to bring our errant behavior, and its causes, into conformity with His laws.

As we allow God to heal our sins and sufferings, as we are giving up control to God to tear down all the walls between us, then we really begin to enjoy an immeasurable trust in God, a great reduction in anxiety and much more peace. Now we begin to enjoy God as we experience Him, because we now have a living relationship with Him.

Illumination

As God hands down His commandments and then laws through Moses, He is beginning our process of *illumination*, the third stage of the classic spiritual journey. For it is in the longer forty years in the wilderness after the drama on Mt. Sinai that God begins to teach us how to be a follower of His ways and Kingdom. The most important element of the illumination period is that we have quit our rebellion against God. The worship of other gods, the wrestling back of control of our lives, our tendency to go off on our own ideas, our addictions, our ignorance of God's ways—all have to go so that God can bring us to a place of illumination, to fulfill our purpose, to work hand-in-hand with God in His created agenda for us, to work with our gifts and talents to serve God through serving others. Here in this long journey through the wilderness we are dealing with all our unconscious assumptions, expectations and preferences. When they are transformed, aligned with God's, then we are in the illumination stage. We still maintain our identity in the world, but are close to giving that up.

Towards the end of the wilderness journey, near the banks of the Jordan River, we learn how to be totally connected to God in all things—that is, in unceasing prayer and in absolute trust. We no longer rebel. We come into the ripeness of who we are, now able to express the fruit of the Spirit—"love, joy, peace, forbearance, kindness, goodness, faithfulness, gentleness, and self-control."[8] These are the signs of a maturing love of God, of a deep relationship with Him, of the Indwelling Spirit of God leading us. We are learning how to bring our lives totally under God's authority by following the thrust of the Ten Commandments and the Law as Jesus summarized in the Two Great Commandments. [9]

---

[8] Galatians 5:22-3
[9] Matthew 22:36-40

15

It is at the end of the wilderness journey that we come into enough of God's influence that we see the clear consequences of our actions—blessings if we follow God's laws and curses if we don't.[10] We also see clearly our purpose and how to carry that out. Just as Joshua and Caleb were free of rebellion, by the time we reach the cross-over point to the Kingdom, the River Jordan, we will have been healed of our rebellious ways, transformed into people who are deeply in communion with God, and deeply obedient to His plans. We are still in the world, but much less of the world.

Union

And now we are ready to enter the Promised Land, the Kingdom of God where all needs are met, and all challenges resolved in God's ways. This is the time of *union* with God, where God's Word and we are one. We follow His suggestions, not out of obedience, but out of love. We know that He has a plan for all the difficult problems we will encounter, and there will be many. But if we follow His plan, like the Israelites did in Jericho and beyond, we will prevail; God's Kingdom will prevail. This new territory is rich in soil and produce for all our needs and will provide our descendants and us with a wonderful land for centuries. There will be challenges and entrenched interests, but as we adhere to God's plan for us, we will be successful in reclaiming these territories.

While this Exodus story was of an outer adventure through the wilderness for the Israelites, for us it becomes an

---

[10] Deuteronomy 28, the entire chapter outlines the blessings and curses

inner journey deep within ourselves to where God is the center of our lives. Egypt, the wilderness and Canaan all exist within us. Here are all the very human tendencies within us that have to be quelled, not by force, but by the Holy Spirit's transforming powers, and then incorporated into our growing-in-God-selves. Each and every "tribe" and "people" in the land of Canaan represent parts of ourselves that resist God and His providence. And so, our lives are consumed with the conversion of the "heathen" within us, so that we can be totally at one with God. Another way to state this is that we are being converted to the mind of Christ. So that we will think like Christ thinks.

It is a long journey with God, transforming us along the way, from awakening to union. As we travel, we begin to experience the freedom of being who we were created to be. As we cross the River Jordan we are free now of the constraints of the world's ways; we are free just to be who we are in God, doing what He has freed us to do, resting in His arms forever.

You may recognize in the stages of awakening, purgation, illumination and union, the normal stages of a transition well-accomplished. We may be fired from a job, have to exist in limbo for a while as we figure out what to do next, may have to train for a whole new occupation or give up our rebellion with what has happened, or find a new way to deal with our changed life. Then finally, we are off in a whole new direction, to a whole new life. This book is about a transition, surely, but the ultimate one from being enslaved to the world's ways to living in God's Kingdom, a total conversion of the way we live.

In this book, I will be referencing the Exodus story in Exodus, Leviticus, Numbers, Deuteronomy and Joshua, but I will not be retelling that story in detail. Each part of this book will begin with citations of the passages covered, so that you can refer to them to jog your memory about the story or to read it perhaps for the first time. There will be summaries of the key points in each part of the story. Some parts of the story are well-known, like the plagues and the Israelites leaving Egypt and the handing down of the Ten Commandments on Mount Sinai. Other stories are not so familiar to us, like all the laws in Leviticus, Numbers and Deuteronomy. But, by looking up the references, you will be up to speed.

The laws handed down to the Israelites through these three books, plus Exodus and Joshua, are appropriate to the history of the times—about animals, husbandry and crops, neighbors and foreigners, God and worshipping Him. The laws that God would hand down to us detailing how He wants us to be with Him will be given to each of us in a step-by-step process of revealing which issues now need to be addressed in us in the context of the 21st century. They would cover the same areas of our lives, our work, our marriages, our friends and neighbors, their property, our leisure time, how to worship, etc.—all of who we are and the principles by which we should live.

Exodus is a beautiful story, compelling and dynamic. It will teach us all we need to know to brave the adventure of leaving our own place of slavery. Thus, enabling the closing of the door on slavery, coupled with the intervening years in the wilderness, that will eventually open another door in Canaan for us, which is the land of milk and honey where all our needs are provided. We'll look at some of the detail of the Exodus story, the laws and commandments, the reactions of the Israelites, the promises that God makes to us—we'll examine this story in some of its wonderful detail in order to see the plan God has laid out for us. Come along with me and see what God is inviting you and me, all of us, to do and to be.

I never thought I would be so fascinated by the whole sweep of this story. But obviously, the Holy Spirit felt differently. For the last four or five years I have been reading these five books, thinking about them, incorporating what they teach us into my life and, finally, coming to this idea of the Exodus story being God's template for us all. Of course, that idea was the Holy Spirit's. I write with His inspiration. All error is mine; all truth is His.

You will be reading illustrations from my own life and from my blog readers at *By the Waters* on Facebook, as well as some Christians from the 19th and 20th centuries. In the spring of 2016 and the winter of 2017, I asked my readers to tell me their stories that fit into this template. The stories from my readers (who will remain anonymous) will help me picture for you how what I am writing about fits into a person's life. All citations from the Bible in the book are from the New International Version, the NIV, unless otherwise noted.

I am Pat Adams, a spiritual director, supervisor of spiritual directors, blogger about living a life centered in God and the author of *Thy Kingdom Come!* I write with little reference to theology or belief systems. My interest is entirely in how we can live the life that Jesus taught and calls us to live. This book promotes the view of Christianity that Jesus calls us to a whole new life. I think that Jesus was a radical in His day and certainly still is in ours. Few of us come close to living the life He described. I think the Exodus story gives us a very practical way, a template for how we can live the life for which He created us, of course, with His help--He does the heavy lifting of healing and transforming us, as long as we are willing to go where He leads.

Part I: Awakening

Chapter One:

Introduction

(See Exodus, Part I covers chapters 1 - 14)

Introduction to the Template

God is always calling us out of slavery to the world just as He first called Noah to save his life and Abraham to come follow Him into a new land, to dwell in His Kingdom. He is calling us to surrender our place in the world, to leave our attachments in the past, to come live in the present with Him. He is always sowing the seeds of change in us, calling us to our deeper selves, speaking to our souls, calling us to be true to ourselves, and to be true to Him. What is apparent in this first part of the Exodus story is that God does not want us enslaved to anything. He wants us to give over our lives to Him, but willingly, so that we may realize our full potential as human beings, to become the whole person He created each of us to be. He wants us to live life fully, richly and to fulfill our purpose. He needs us giving all that we are to the world in love, so that we might help bring in the Kingdom of God on this Earth. He is the One who knows us so well and all that we could be, if we could leave slavery to the world behind.

The main issue of Part I of the Exodus story where we're still enslaved in our own "Egypt" is this: *Are we going to answer God's invitation to leave behind our attachment to the world's ways, our enslavement to the ego's needs and desires, to embark on a journey into the unknown, following wherever He leads us?* We will see the obstacles that keep us from leaving.

The *awakening* stage of the spiritual journey happens when the soul awakens to God's whispered call. As the person responds more and more to the soul's call, the journey goes deeper and deeper into ourselves, the attachment to God grows, the attachment to the world's ways recedes. This awakening stage requires a surrender of our lives to God, being born again in the Lord. Then trust in God begins in a real way.

Isabella Baumfree, a 19th century slave, escaped her master in 1826 with her infant daughter. She successfully sued her master to recover her son. In 1843 she changed her name to Sojourner Truth. "The Spirit calls me, and I must go," she told her friends. She went on to advocate for the rights of slaves and women, for religious tolerance and pacifism.[11] She answered God's call. She followed where He led her.

---

[11] https://en.wikipedia.org/wiki/Sojourner_Truth#.22The_Spirit_Calls_Me.22, 6.17.16

22

How do we recognize these calls from God? There are numerous ways. First, we have to be still enough inside of us to distinguish God's voice from all the other inner voices. The Indwelling Spirit of God speaks in a "gentle whisper," in a "still, small voice,"[12] so it has to be listened for in order to be heard. It is the voice to which we habitually answer, "Oh, I can't do that!" or "No way, Jose." We need to pay attention to what we are rejecting. Sometimes the suggestions from God come in dreams. These suggestions are offered by our soul, where the Indwelling Spirit of God dwells.

Sometimes the wake-up call happens through a tragic event, the loss of a job, the death of a loved one, a storm or earthquake that destroys our home. We are thrown into the wilderness by the circumstances of our life and given the opportunity to reassess how we are living and whether the way we live is congruent with who we are. There often is no time to choose whether we want to change how we live; we are already in changed circumstances, trying disparately to cope with them.

The first thing to know about the Exodus story is that God's hand is in every action, every call. He notices the agony of the Israelites. He calls Moses back to Egypt to be deliver them. Through Moses He challenges the Pharaoh, even hardening his heart. Through Moses He sends ten plagues, which only affect the Egyptians.[13] When the Israelites finally leave, He directs Moses to part the Red Sea.

---

[12] 1 Kings 19:12 NIV, KJV
[13] Exodus 7:14-Exodus 11 With the 10th plague, the killing of the first-born sons and livestock, God gave specific instructions to the Israelites so their children and livestock would be passed over. Exodus 11-12

Then, He has Moses return the sea to normal as the Egyptian army and the Pharaoh are about half-way across. He is active in the lives of the Israelites, as they prepare to follow the guide He has provided them, Moses.

It does not seem that leaving slavery behind would be difficult at all, but there it is: leaving "Egypt" which stands for the world in this story is fraught with challenges, attachments to the known, fear of the unknown, a lack of trust in the providence of God and more. If we treat this story as our story, we might say that slavery is not such a bad thing. We may moan and groan under the burden of slavery, but we don't recognize it as such. It is the reality we live in and don't notice so much the cost to us of living as slaves.

Slavery can be a state of mind and a physical reality. In the case of the Israelites, it is both.

But what are we 21st century people enslaved to? What the world and our culture offer us is a very narrow view of what life could be. And the lens that we use to look on our own life comes down to this: *What do I have to do to fit into this culture in order to be a success in life?* The lens we're peering through defines us as definitely lacking some basic quality that everyone else seems to have, that only we are lacking.

Contrast that with God's point of view: He loves each and every one of us human beings. He forgives us of our shortcomings and any mistakes we might have made. He can see the person He created us to be and wants to *free* that potential within us, so that we can find fulfillment and purpose on this Earth and be in a close relationship with Him.

At least under the familiar cultural framework, we know what each day will be like. We might have family and friends close by who wouldn't want to go with us—they tie us to the present state of affairs. We might be experiencing a raft of inner voices that all have different agendas, i.e. 1) the inner Pharaoh/ego, the entrenched power, 2) the inner Egyptians who demand that we stay and adhere to the rules of the culture, as well as 3) parts of us that are unhappy being a slave, but fearful of the unknown ahead, 4) an inner Moses, the voice of our soul who would lead us out of the place of slavery speaking for God, calling us to freedom.

Sometimes it is our belief systems that enslave us. If you are a captive of the kind of thinking that puts you down, you are living in Egypt under the Pharaoh. If you've bought into a set of beliefs that describe God as a big man in the sky with a thunderbolt ready to zap you when you sin, as I did, you are a slave to that belief. If you cater to others as more intelligent, more handsome, more deserving than you, you are caught in Egypt. If you believe in a God that doesn't match your experience of God, then your life belongs to what others say about God. If you cannot feel God's love at the cellular level, you are enslaved to thinking that limits what you can take in of God's offer of love and forgiveness. Just believing that you are loved without actually feeling loved does not serve you or the purpose for which you were created.

One of the worst forms of slavery is addiction. Drug and alcohol addictions take over people's lives in obvious ways. Often our lives are totally centered around getting

25

that fix; and we will do anything to fulfill the all-consuming desire. Other addictions are more subtle: to the TV, to games, to the Internet, to social media, to shopping, and more. Addictions focus our attention away from the present to just filling our enormous need right now, to the exclusion of thoughtful approaches to our families, our spouses, our work, our anything. They consume our lives.

Just as the Israelites were slowly enslaved, our own enslavement to the culture, to our upbringing, to our own self-concept and other things evolves gradually, too, in our childhood, long before our cognitive brains are developed. Before we're able to intellectually sort out our experience, we are conditioned by the culture as if we were blank slates, just waiting to be written on. There are many things that children cannot put into context and therefore accept with their limited understanding. As we grow up, we are beginning to forget whatever we knew of our souls and God. As children, we don't realize how long it takes to train a child to the point that s/he needs no more reminders about the rules. Meanwhile we're creating our self-image out of a lot of misunderstandings, especially those about how bad we are and how there is a lot in us that we have to make up for.

Depending on the child and the family, this training to be obedient can take six to ten or more years. With every failure to obey, the child experiences guilt and shame after, say, the age of 4 or 5. As these experiences of our failures to obey once again add up, they color our self-concept negatively. And that is in a good family. If there is a lot of anger or abuse, then the message the child gets is a lot worse. At some young age, each child decides how life is for him or her, how he or she must live in the world. A child might decide a number of different ways depending on his /her experience. He might decide that life won't work out for him, or that she has to badger everyone until they give her what she wants, or that the shame is too great to. . ., or he's too afraid to or too angry to. . . , or any variation on these themes.

This self-concept is set long before we have the ability to truly see the truth of who we are in this world, and how much God wants us to be free of anything that enslaves us. That big and largely unconscious decision drives all our decision-making long into adulthood and maybe for the rest of our lives, if we never become conscious of it. And so we enslave ourselves because of the guilt and shame we experienced in our upbringing.

Fortunately, if we conceded to the slavery of our negative self-image as children, we can also as mature adults dis-enslave ourselves. God is always calling us out of slavery and into the Kingdom. Listen to what He is speaking to you. It may scare you to follow that voice, but it will lead to greater freedom and to love.

We can be enslaved to money, material things, comfort, addictions—which mostly keep us from facing the pain and suffering in our lives. We can be enslaved to a certain person, to a job, to fear or anger that we wouldn't survive if we left "Egypt", to resignation—there's no way out! This slavery often involves how we think; it comes down to decisions about ourselves that we made as young children without our knowledge. These ways of slavery branch out and infiltrate our self-esteem, adhering to the culture, to being independent and more, even to the letter of the law, to "gobs of gods."

Once I had left my own version of "Egypt" by surrendering my life to God, I spent three days walking on air. Then I came crashing down to Earth with this on my mind: "Thou shalt have no other gods before me!" I wrote for days listing all the gods/things/people that I put before God in my life: other's opinions of me, an addiction to sugar, doubt of myself, lack of trust in God and pages more. I called that list, "gobs of gods."

What we are enslaved to becomes a cloudy lens through which we look at God and life; we can only see what we expect to see, denying all other possibilities. We can only see a small part of who God is and that is often distorted by our projections on Him. And we only see the neediest part of ourselves and focus on that.

There is nothing that the culture or the world offers us that can free us—not more money, not a prettier wife or richer husband or a better car. We have to go all the way with God and let Him transform our ways and especially our minds, so that we can see and know what is true and real.

The first part of the template we see in the Exodus story is our own slavery to our own self-concept, to the world and to the culture we live in. And there is God hearing our cries of pain as the burden is doubled.

So, our first task is to say "Yes!" to God's invitation to leave the place of slavery. We say "Yes!" to God's ways, "Yes!" to Him leading us, "Yes!" to His timing. And more.

Part I: Awakening

Chapter Two

God, Egypt and the Israelites

God hears the cries of His people, and calls Moses to partnership

The Lord called Moses to lead the Israelites out of slavery. Moses had been in exile in Midian. As we know from the story of Moses in the bulrushes,[14] he was born into an Israelite household, raised by Pharaoh's daughter as her own. As an adult, he had fled to Midian because he killed an Egyptian whom he witnessed tormenting an Israelite.[15] In Midian God appeared to Moses in a burning bush, told him he was on hallowed ground, to remove his sandals. "So now, go. I am sending you to Pharaoh to bring my people the Israelites out of Egypt."[16] Moses asked who was sending

---

[14]Exodus 2:1-10
[15] Exodus 2:11-12
[16] Exodus 3:1-10

him? "I Am who I Am," God replies.[17] And so, God is calling us, too, through our inner Moses, to follow God's lead, to leave our slavery to the world, so that we may come to rest in the I Am who I Am.

Moses who represents our soul is calling us to listen to the Lord, to follow His instructions, to get out of slavery:

"I have heard the groaning of the Israelites, whom the Egyptians are enslaving, and I have remembered my covenant. Therefore, say to the Israelites: 'I am the LORD, and I will bring you out from under the yoke of the Egyptians. I will free you from being slaves to them, and I will redeem you with an outstretched arm and with mighty acts of judgment. I will take you as my own people, and I will be your God. Then you will know that I am the LORD your God, who brought you out from under the yoke of the Egyptians. And I will bring you to the land I swore with uplifted hand to give to Abraham, to Isaac and to Jacob. I will give it to you as a possession. I am the LORD.'"[18]

In Part I of the Exodus story we see all kinds of hurdles to leaving Egypt. The Pharaoh prompted by God gets more hard-hearted every day; even with all the plagues God sends his way, he just becomes more adamant.[19] Pharaoh's cold-hearted attitude towards the Israelites is going to make it easier for them eventually to leave Egypt.

The Indwelling Spirit of God, which sees reality, calls us out of slavery. The Spirit calls our inner Moses and Aaron, tells them what to do and when—how to break the

---

[17] Exodus 3:14
[18] Exodus 6:5-8
[19] Exodus 10:1-2

bonds. At the same time, He is hardening Pharaoh's heart to not let us go. Thus, the battle of the ego—Pharaoh--and the true self/soul begins.

God is visible only in the plagues and in what Moses tells the Israelites in this part of the story. Later, He will be visible day and night. God, who has given us free will to choose the trajectory of our lives and every detail, too, sees the condition of our lives here: the limitations, the pain, the falseness of the thinking, our suffering and calls us out of our enslavement to the way the world and way human cultures' think. He does not want us to live in these circumstances.

The Exodus story is God's way of showing us that there is a way out, a template for following Him to freedom by loving and being obedient to Him, so that we might live in the Promised Land, a land that easily meets our needs, a land that is the Kingdom of God. While He invites the Israelites to a physical land, Canaan, the Kingdom is not a physical place, it is a state of mind where we all find our true home, a true community, a place of rest, refreshment and where we live out our purpose to serve God in the world. The first of the major points I will make about the Exodus story is that God is calling us out of Egypt throughout our lives, out of our enslavement to the world into His Kingdom.

If God had wanted to create obedient people who would never stray from His laws and from His side, He would have created us without free will. Instead, He gave us that freedom and wants us to come to Him willingly. There is no way that He did not know that we would be a disobedient, inconstant creation of His. He, who designed

31

some 7 plus million species[20] for the planet Earth alone, who created an interdependent system in which each species could thrive, who could design in such incredible detail, could not have been surprised at the way we turn out.

The circumstances of slavery were not the vision He held for our lives here. He calls us out of Egypt that we might enjoy His plan for us here on Earth, right now. Metaphorically, He calls forth our "inner" Moses who would lead us out of slavery. He speaks to us through His Indwelling Spirit, offering ideas and suggestions that, if followed, would begin to break up our dependence on and attachment to the world. He dangles before us in a myriad of ways the Land of Canaan, the place where all our needs are met. He sows seeds in us of invitation to a wholly different kind of life than the one we have now. And He uses, but doesn't cause, difficult circumstances in our lives to offer a redemptive way of life, not a return to the problematic one we led before.

And so, He offers us this story of the Israelites who went from being slaves in Egypt through the long trek in the wilderness to the Promised Land, to the Kingdom. It contains all that we need to know to follow our own inner "Moses" who would lead us with God out of slavery into a much more integrated, integral life, the life He designed for us at our creation. The Exodus story is a rich template of the steps we need to take and what we need to learn as we travel the road to freedom.

---

[20] www.currentresults.com/Environment-Facts/Plants-Animals/estimate-of-worlds-total-number-of-species.php

Read how the Rev. Steve Garnass-Holmes describes God in poetry:

My child,
do you know how much I love you?

I give you everything,
all that I have, all Creation.
It breaks my heart
when you turn away —
how many times a day? —
but I love you,
and I will give myself to you.
Come to me.

You may go to a far land or out into the field;
however far off you are I will see you.
I will come to you, shaking with love.
I will leave the party to come to you.
I will hike my robe up around my knees,
running foolishly, to come to you.
Do you know how I weep with joy?
Come home.

Rebellious or obedient, you are my Beloved.
I will silence your speech about just desserts.
I will ignore the wise advisors,
foolishly, extravagantly, over and over
I will offer you my best.
I will give you myself.
Come in.

Though you have turned from your brother
I will give you back to each other.
You who are dead to one another I will restore.
I will give you back your family.
I will bring you back to life,
give you back to myself.

When you break my heart again
I will still love you, still give you myself,
again and again forever, for the sake of love.
Come in,
for our sake.[21]

God lives for the day we will turn to Him and leave behind the ways of the world. What He holds out for us is a life in which He takes care of all of our needs. [22]I know some would say that God doesn't need us, but then why would He send His only Son as the invitation to a greater life in Him? Through Jesus, He establishes what needs to happen first: "Seek first his kingdom and his righteousness, and all these things will be given to you as well." [23] So our part is to put God first in our lives and then all will be given to us that we need for sustenance, for our physical needs, for our spiritual needs, for our purpose, for everything, especially for an abundant life.

---

[21]Rev. Steve Garnaas-Holmes, www.unfoldinglight.net
[22]Psalms 23:1, Luke 12:7 and more.
[23]Matthew 6:33

Leaving Egypt—a place of slavery to the world

Let's now look at the country of Egypt. This is a country bisected by the River Nile, which floods the adjacent lands and keeps the land arable and rich. Egypt is an ancient country, a cradle of civilization, going as far back as the 10th millennium B.C. Most of the people lived right along the Nile River, because the rest of the land is Saharan.

Metaphorically, Egypt stands for the world, the place where we are enslaved. Just like the Israelites who first came to Egypt freely and later became slaves to the Pharaoh, our inner Pharaoh/ego gradually assumes power over us as we grow up as children and mature into adults. We forget who created us and our natural created self, and opt to follow this ruler/ego, no matter how abusive he is.

As we read the Exodus story, we can see how difficult it is to leave a place of slavery, of comfort in a known world; we see our unwillingness to take a risk and to try something new. It is far easier for us to conform to the world than to leave it, even when the world is not a good fit for us. We may resist the pressures of our society, we may groan under its burdens, but we don't think of leaving it behind. The Exodus story is one of physical movement from Egypt to Canaan, but the story I am telling is about an inner journey of complete conversion from living in the world's ways to living in God and His ways.

What makes us recognize that we are enslaved? What moves us out of slavery? What makes us walk away to reclaim our lives as our own? What in your life has called you to greater freedom? To your own true self? What is God whispering to you? What aspect of your true self wants to emerge and find a foothold in your life? What calls us to greater life can range from a disaster like Katrina, where everything is lost, to a simple voice inside you that grabs your attention to a feeling that you just can't take it anymore and may not even know what the "it" is that is so disempowering and dispiriting.

C_____, a reader of my Facebook blog, wrote that she had a head-on collision with a drunk driver when he drove into her lane. She suffered several injuries and lost most of her memory, yet she awoke with a grateful heart to God's voice saying this: "I will never leave you or forsake you." Later her memory returned and she was healed. She has never ever asked God, "Why? Why me? Why this accident?" Because of several other storms in the past that she was able to heal with God's help, she has just learned to surrender all "when the winds and waves and storms come."

For me it was a voice within that shocked me, "I have an agenda for my life!" I was such a product of the 1940's and 50's that in my early 40's when I heard that sentence, I was inhabiting roles—wife, mother, volunteer—and had no idea who the "I" was that had an agenda, much less what the agenda was. Hearing that sentence started me on a long journey of self-discovery, now asking constantly, "What do I *really* want to do?" instead of following the many voices of "shoulds" which had ruled my life up to then. And then, along came a time within a year or two, I surrendered my life to God. And then I entered the wilderness.

That voice telling me that there was something more I was to do, the voice of God's Indwelling Spirit, called me out of slavery to all that I had learned from our culture up until then. Just like God sent Moses to the Israelites, one of their own, to lead them out of slavery to the Egyptians, He calls us to greater life,[24] to our own true selves as He created us to be, to a deep relationship with Him.

As I read the stories of survivors of Hurricane Katrina today, I am struck by how losing everything brought them new life, eventually. One young man, Shawn Kelly, who was ten years old at the time the storm came, moved with his family to Dallas where the schools were so much better that they helped instill in him a love of learning and achieving. He is currently a junior at Loyola College. Another child (at the time) moved with his family to an apartment where Sam Williams, a New Orleans trombonist, lived with them. It was listening to Sam practice all the time that inspired John Bradford to learn to play the trumpet. He is now an up-and-coming musician at age 19.[25]

Sometimes life is just like that: it takes you out of one place and dumps you in another. Or an inner voice may call you. Or there may be a general sense that there is something more. There are all kinds of ways that we are moved out of slavery. And then there is the transition, the wilderness, between slavery and the new life. We'll talk about that in Part II. For now we're still enslaved.

Israelites

The Israelites represent all human beings who are slaves to the world, to the culture in which they live. They represent the part of us that doesn't want change, that wants

---

[24] John 10:10 "I have come that they may have life, and have it to the full."
[25] www.mtv.com/news/2249128/young-katrina-survivors-remember-storm/ 2.19.16

to keep things the way they were. That doesn't want to deal with pain or challenge. That always just wants things to go back to "normal" whatever that was. (I have found "normal" to be an ever-changing target.)

Just like the Israelites, let us acknowledge that we, too, are slaves to our culture, a social system that is very different from our created nature, maybe even the opposite of what God had in mind for us when we were created. Our American culture has a way of doing and being in this world that extols self-sufficiency, that depends on a direct approach to everything, that promotes each of us seeking what we need or what our family needs to the exclusion of everyone else, that focuses on succeeding at goal after goal, that blames the poor for their problems, and more. "As long as I and mine are taken care of. . . well, then it's okay." "As long as I fit myself into the American mold. . . well, then it's okay."

So, when we contemplate leaving "Egypt," what are we leaving behind? We are shedding any attachments to the culture, especially the culture's way of being and thinking, and even our own ways of being and thinking. We are relinquishing our dependence on the outer world to set our agendas and our insistence on our own will being primary. We are giving up our own self-centeredness and the "normal" way of doing and being. We may be admitting addictions to substances as well as strict patterns of thinking, repetitive escape avenues like dependence on electronics, TV, books and other things to avoid confronting ourselves. We are surrendering our flight from pain and suffering, guilt and shame. Most of all, I think we are giving up our attachments and our preferences in favor of what is real and true.

When I asked my blog readers for examples of leaving Egypt, most examples I got were of recovery from addictions to drugs and alcohol. These addictions which help us escape feeling our own pain and suffering are just the worst examples of running from our images of ourselves. D____ is a good example of a recovering addict. "I was broken in every way possible. I had been in active addiction in and out for 22 years" when she was brought to a retreatment center. "It was here I learned I had a disease...[that] God could and would [help me] if He were sought...I surrendered fully to His will. And [I] learned and [I am] still learning and becoming the woman God intended me to be." She now works in that treatment center and helps others. "Four years plus four months of sobriety!"

What do we have to let go of in order to leave Egypt? We have to say yes to God, so we are giving up all our own plans, etc., in favor of a life putting God first. First of all, Egypt is our normal context, the familiar; it's what we are used to. So we have to be willing to try out a new way of living in a new place. Second, we are used to acting out of our culture's priorities for family, work, and leisure. We are used to an outer authority. We do have an inner conscience, but the outer authority and our adherence to it can outweigh our own sensibilities. We humans don't like change much, unless we are the ones initiating it. We not only have to change, but we need to be adaptable, resilient because we no longer know what the future will be like.

Part I: Awakening

Chapter Three

Leaving Slavery, Plagues

How do we get out of slavery?

There are many ways to decide to leave Egypt. We might be answering God's call, allowing the seeds of freedom to grow in us. Or maybe in the natural course of things, we see our lives unravel before our eyes. It might be a recession like the one in 2008-9 which takes your heating business from 40 trucks and crews down to 2 as a recent contractor of mine related. Interestingly, when it first happened, he decided to retire, did chores around the house for a couple of years. But then he was bored and now he commands a crew of two trucks and their crews and is content in that.

It might be a Tsunami which dislodges us from our home and life and lands us in another area of our country. It might be the death of a spouse, loss of income or a child's death. Suddenly, we are transported to another set of priorities that dismiss the attachments we had before. Then we have a choice to reprioritize our lives or to go back the slave state.

I've long thought that a young adult who had some tragedy in their life as they grew up was fortunate in this way: If a parent had died or they were really ill, for example, they would be wrenched off the mindless track that all our children and teens are on to succeed at all cost. They would have to step off the cultural "train" for a while due to the circumstances, but those circumstances would give them a chance to see what was happening in their lives and to re-examine them in light of the new reality. They would have a chance in their grief or in a hospital stay to see other possibilities for themselves. Then, when they recovered, they could get back on the track, but no longer as mindlessly as before. They would be able to choose whether they wanted to be there or not and what they would buy into and what they wouldn't.

Not so for the rest of us! It's like our culture shoots our children as arrows out of the same bow and expects us to land in the same way. This one-size-fits-all culture just doesn't fit most people, but still we adhere to what we were taught, even as adults. To me this is enslavement as bad as the Pharaoh in Egypt at the time of the Israelites and Moses. Our dilemma is the same as the battered wife who cannot imagine living without the man who "loves me." She puts up with all his abuse and stays. No matter that he might kill her someday, "He 'loves' me. He told me so after he calmed down."She can't imagine living a life away from him, an idea he has long promoted. And so, she stays.

Here's a story from E___ who used methamphetamines for thirty years. She was a non-believer who had a nervous breakdown. She screamed out one night: "If there is a God show me, remove this urge for meth, give me my mind back! The next morning I had no urge for meth! With the help of medical professions, I can actually use my mind again, and [I am] giving my life to God, I am a believer." SC

Sometimes God comes in dreams, like this example from F___, another reader. "I was at the peak of my agnostic life. In this dream I was overwhelmed with crisis and chaos. I entered a building. On the inside was a carpenter's shop and a man standing inside working wood. He looked up and our eyes met. I knew there was something about him; I was moving closer to him. His presence was calm, warm, and pure. Words can't truly convey it. He spoke to me. He knew my name (without me telling him). At this point…I knew something profound was happening, but I was still whirling and confused. He looked at me and he told me, quietly, 'Everything is going to be fine, you'll see…' I don't know how long I stayed there (time moves differently in dreams). But when I left [the building], his prophecy was true. The chaos of the dream was resolved and dissolved systematically and the dream ended, leaving me with a strong sense of understanding. This man who was a carpenter, who knew my name, who glowed with love, and prophesied my well-being was HIM: Jesus Christ. I woke up that morning with my life completely changed."

It is not that saying "Yes!" to God, that we will follow Him out of slavery, actually results in our faithful attendance on His word. Sometimes, as my reader, H____, discovered that "Yes!" is a beginning, but the real conversion comes later, after the rebellion is done. While she was converted at a young age, it was a long time before she committed herself 100% to God. In her own words, "I refuse to let Jesus bear the cross alone. I choose to pick up my cross and follow Jesus. I live the 10 Commandments the best I can and the fruit of the Spirit within these commandments. I get so excited talking about Jesus; I am going to serve the Lord in righteousness, because I know one day it will pay off. I know what prayers can do. Prayers have seen me through. I know I have a friend in Jesus. He's my Stronghold and my Battle Axe in time of need. I wouldn't trade him for all the riches in the world. Wealth is temporary; heaven is forever." It takes a long time in the wilderness before our rebelliousness has died out.

Plagues

At least the Israelites knew they were slaves, but it took God's agent, Moses, and his spokesman and brother, Aaron, to call the Israelites out of slavery, to break the bonds that the Pharaoh and the Egyptians—read the culture or world--had on them. By calling on God's power Moses first turned his staff into a snake, which the Pharaoh's magicians could also do. Moses' staff/snake then ate the magicians' snakes! Then Moses called forth ten plagues, which got at the roots of the hold the Egyptians had on the Hebrews.

The blood in the Nile River would destroy the arability of the land. The pests—frogs, gnats, swarms of flies, distracted the people. A plague on the livestock—horses, donkeys, camels, cattle, sheep and goats, the source of wealth and food, killed them. Then festering boils broke out on the people and the animals that were left. A hailstorm with thunder and lightning destroyed many crops. And a plague of locusts ate the rest. Then darkness fell over the land for three days, a darkness that could be felt. Throughout all these plagues, the Pharaoh would say he would let the people go, then change his mind. Or he might let the men go, but no one else. And then changed his mind. Until the last plague, in which the first-born sons of the Egyptians and first-born of the livestock were killed, then the Pharaoh and the Egyptians were glad to see them go— who knew what the next plague would attack?

The Hebrews were given a plan by God to save them from this last plague—to kill a lamb, to paint its blood on the lintel of their doors, to cook and eat all of the lamb that night. The angel of death who was to kill the children under two years of age then "passed" over the houses with blood painted on the lintel. The Pharaoh let them go after that— men, women, children, livestock. They took their neighbors' gold and jewelry with them, which the Egyptians were glad to give them, if it would end the plagues. But when Pharaoh realized what he was losing—the source of his wealth and power-- he and his army chased them down to the Red Sea. The Pharaoh and his army were killed as they tried to cross the Red Sea following the Israelites. The Egyptian army represents the persistence of the hold that slavery has on our thinking, which remains even as we leave the land of slavery.

The Bible relates that God is hardening Pharaoh's heart even as Moses is trying to get him to let his people go, "so that I may perform these signs of mine among them that you may tell your children and grandchildren how I dealt harshly with the Egyptians and how I performed my signs among them, and that you may know that I am the Lord."[26] The plagues certainly make great stories that have come down through the ages of God caring so much for the Israelites, His people, that He prodded the Egyptians to let them go by plagues that were increasingly harmful to the captors. The Pharaoh and the Egyptians stand in this story for the entrenched interests within us, the ego, the old voices out of our childhood which are still trying to keep us on the straight and narrow cultural path, so that we have a place in this world. They are all about the world and how everyone is to behave here.

When we grow up in a culture that we have been indoctrinated into, we may not even realize the hold it has on us. We may not know who we are outside of that culture, because we think the way the culture thinks, we do what the culture says is the right thing to do, we cling to those ways because they are so well known to us; they are habitual.

Jesus said, "No man can serve two masters...Ye cannot serve God and mammon"[27] (read the world). So if we adhere to the cultural standards, we are violating God's. This is the whole reason for a spiritual journey in Christ—we are to move from operating as if the world's version of things were all there is to life to living in God's Kingdom where His "love, joy, peace, patience, goodness, gentleness, kindness, faithfulness and self-control"—the fruit of the

---

[26] Exodus 10:1-2
[27] Matthew 6:24 KJV

46

Spirit[28]—reign. And it takes a long time for that conversion to happen—forty years for the Israelites, 3 years for Paul of Tarsus, a similar time for the disciples of Jesus. And for the rest of us, all I know is that it has taken me 30 years after I surrendered my life to Christ to not be able to tell where the Holy Spirit ends and I begin. I can't now see any difference. It took that many years of following the "still, small voice"[29] to an integrated, natural life for me.

What do we experience when we leave tradition or patterns that used to serve us well? A chorus of voices saying, "You can't do that!" I lived in a nice neighborhood in Northern California for 38 years with a tax-payer subsidized swimming pool and nice neighbors. A middle-to-upper-middle class neighborhood. Next to us was a wealthy community with 1 to 2.5 acre minimums. When one of our neighbors moved to the wealthier community, they really got criticized by their old neighbors. So it is with family, friends and neighbors, when we make a different choice. The chorus of naysayers is huge and loud. The sense of betrayal is huge. They might as well be saying, "A plague on you!"

I talked to a woman recently who was talking too much to others about an issue in her life. She knew what God was saying to her about it, but her friends and family were trying to keep her where she was-- in anxiety. So she was torn between following God's wisdom and having peace in her circle of close friends and family. Her doubts about God's wisdom came from all around her. How could she move out of Egypt with them pulling her back?

---

[28]Galatians 5:22-3
[29]1 Kings 19:12 KJV

And then there are the consequences from our own negative tapes within us—You can't do that! You should stay! You need to wait until the time is ripe! You're supposed to _____! The chorus of naysayers within us is legion. The ego does not like change. It does not like any threat to its power over us. The call of the soul is often just to a very subtle disengagement with what is, one small step at a time, but the ego denies it, talks loudly over it, undermines it. Our inner landscape echoes what we are hearing from our family and friends and the culture.

What do we make of the plagues, the measures God takes to disengage us from the power of the slave master, the Pharaoh? We could see them as taking away the Pharaoh's grip on our thinking and emotions, destroying the crops and riches that sustain the Egyptians, whittling away at the power that they hold over us. None of the plagues touched the Israelites, but helped them leave and disengage from the beleaguered Egyptians.

After my husband died it took me a few years to disengage from our home of twenty-eight years. First I moved from the Peninsula forty minutes north to an apartment in San Francisco while my future daughter-in-law lived in our home. I stayed there for nine months until I realized that I had no desire to meet people there, to make friends or get involved in the community. I was still traveling down to the Peninsula to see friends, to go to church, etc. Then I moved back to the Peninsula and rented an apartment there. Finally, after two years I was able to get the house ready to sell. Then I was finally able to deal with all the "stuff" we had collected in 37 years of marriage—more attachments.

Sometimes our attachments result from severe unhappiness and dysfunction in our upbringing. J____ grew up in a paradoxical family: her mother a Christian, her father an abuser. And she herself was so emotional, she "felt sorry for everyone. I would give away everything I had. Yet I did not make people happy by giving it all away." She was full of heartache until one day she had an epiphany: "I realized that I Could Not Fix The World. My Duty was to Obey One Person. Jesus Christ. I [had been] One person that Had to Live Around people; I could not be alone. [After] God gave me my Peace, I now live in the country. So at peace."

In any issue we face, we have to disengage from the old, the past, expect to be in limbo for a while, until we can learn a new way of being, but that is the story of Parts II and III.

What sacrifices do we have to make to leave "slavery," and the hold on us that the world/culture/friends/family have? It's not that we're leaving them behind, just the power they have over us. To whom will we be true? To all the outside influences? To our own true selves? To God? Who is going to govern us? This is a death, a crucifixion, if you will, in which we die to the past in order to move into the present where we can meet God.

We waffle. We decide to go. Then we decide to stay. It is so difficult to decide against all the ego is telling us in order to follow our own soul and God. It's difficult to face our family's and friends' objections and still leave. It's really tough to leave Egypt.

One can judge the power that the world has over us— how strong our attachment to it is—by how many and how awful the plagues were that finally set the Israelites free. We are beholden to the parts of us who won't let us go. It takes ten plagues for the Pharaoh to let go and then the Pharaoh/ego chases after us trying to convince us that we are wrong in leaving them! That they need us! That we won't survive without them, and many other arguments.

The question for all of us is this: *To whom will we be true? All these outside influences? To our own true selves? To God? Who is it to be who governs us?*

Part I: Awakening

Chapter Four:

Cast of Characters, Freedom, Suffering

Cast of Characters

The first thing we notice in the cast of characters is that none of the humans was a perfect man. Certainly not the Pharaoh who spoke out of both sides of his mouth, who said whatever he thought would help him keep his power. Nor was Moses, an Israelite, a perfect man. He grew up in the Pharaoh's household; he had killed an Egyptian and was not a great speaker. Aaron, his brother, was a fine speaker, but eventually helped the Israelites construct an idol to another god, Ba'al. And even God in this story was mostly faithful to His promises, but there was an instance later on in the story where God was so upset with the Israelites' inconstancy that Moses had to remind Him to be true to His own covenants.[30]

Moses is the part of us who has already left Egypt or never really belonged to the world. He is not attached to it. Moses was born an Israelite, raised by the Pharaoh's daughter who has been living in Midian because he had to flee punishment for killing an Egyptian who was abusing a Jew. The Lord is calling Moses, that is, the part of us that can communicate with God, that is not identified with being a Hebrew or an Egyptian or a Midianite, to lead us out of slavery.[31]

Moses is calling us to listen to the Lord, to follow His instructions, to get out of Egypt. In Part I of the Exodus story we see all kinds of hurdles to leaving Egypt. The Pharaoh, prompted by God got more hard-hearted every day, even with all the plagues God sent his way, he just became more and more adamant that the Israelites stay.

Pharaoh/ego represents the entrenched power in us largely set in our childhood, which doesn't want to change, which becomes more and more adamant, clinging to power even as the plagues threaten him and his rule. Pharaoh is called by God to become more hard-hearted. And why would that be? Because we need to see how tyrannical the ruler is, how uncaring he is of our circumstances and well-being, how disdainful he is of our true selves, our souls, so that we will finally decide to leave his power over us behind. God eggs him on with worse and worse plagues and more and more obstinacy. For us the Pharaoh's voice would be the

---

[30] Exodus 33:3
[31] Exodus 3:10

one that clings to the known and to his power over us. He fears the unknown.

We could see the Pharaoh as the inner representative of the culture in which we live: he's the one who keeps us in line, who ignores the urgings of our soul for authenticity, who enslaves us to laws and to work that don't satisfy, who keeps us wanting to make more and more money so that we can buy more and more stuff, who will not free us, because we do so much for him. He is the ego's ready partner, enslaving us to the things of this world.

Freedom

As we delve into this ancient story, we need to first consider what freedom God is offering us. As Americans, we have freedom of religion, the freedom to move wherever we want, to seek any job we want, the right to vote as we please, to pursue our own brand of happiness. What more could God offer us? How about the freedom to be who He created us to be which is the freedom to live in integrity and authenticity. The freedom to pursue and to fulfill our own purpose. The freedom to love. The freedom to belong to a bigger, more loving community. The freedom to give of ourselves to the Kingdom. The freedom to find our own true home in God's arms. This freedom that God offers is not the freedom to do anything we want for our own selfish desires. If we are living in the freedom that God has promised, we are to give ourselves back to the world as we have been given to. This freedom is extended for the good of all, for God's Kingdom, out of gratitude for all we've been given.

Our political and social freedoms and God's spiritual freedom are very different. Our democratic freedoms are a step up from all the lack of freedoms in more restrictive countries, but nothing like the freedom that God offers us to just be ourselves. To be loved and forgiven for who we are. To be a partner of the One who created us, who knows us better than we know ourselves. To no longer wear the masks of the society that we live in demands. To fulfill our purpose. Finally, we can relax and be our own true selves.

The amazing thing for me and why I have been so faithful to God all these years is that whatever the Holy Spirit has suggested that I do has been affirming of my deepest self and has always worked out in my best interests and for those I am close to. I call this period the 10,000 surrenders, because there are literally tons of surrenders everyday of my will, my assumptions, my expectations, my preferences—all world-based-- in the face of what is before me. Sometimes, I cry out to God, teasing Him, "What were you thinking when you brought this thing or person into my life!" But then, I let go of my will and learn how to be with what is. And that is just the small stuff. After 20 years of practicing surrender to everything small, I was able to do the same with my husband's cancer and death, because I no longer wanted to say "no" to God. I had learned to trust that inner voice, to know that whether Hank lived or died that I would be fine and that he also would be fine. I would grieve, but, in the end, I would adapt to this new reality.

The resistance to leaving "Egypt" is our own. It's about our own inner "Pharaoh" and the other "Egyptian" voices that would keep us right where we are, where there is no unknown territory or conditions, where we are "safe," at least according to our own voices. These voices are noisy and disruptive of anything they don't like, so it takes quite a bit of quieting down our minds, so that we can hear God's whisper.[32] It takes an ability to step back from our own thinking objectively and to see the old sources of this thinking. I hear my mother and father's voice in my insistence on being on time whenever I am going anywhere. Even when I am obviously going to be early, I can be anxious about being on time. Or I hear my mother going on about having poise in social situations. Or my Aunt Grace who could not stay on a long-distance call, even if I was paying for it, for more than a minute. She had little money to waste. Or my Father's mantra to his children: "The Lord helps those who help themselves."

Rarely are these voices appropriate now; these are the voices that were incorporated internally to keep you on track when you were a child and having trouble following the rules, as children do. But today they cause havoc in our lives because, in their clamor to be heard, they drown out the legitimate self, the deep-soul self, which holds the agenda for our lives. That is also the voice of the Indwelling Spirit of God. We have to step back from these childhood voices, see them for what they are, and listen for the deeper inner voice, which rings true to our souls. This is the original surrender to our own true selves, which God created us to be. He gave us gifts and talents, and even challenges to overcome, so that we might someday come into our own and do what we were created to do: To make the Kingdom visible on this Earth.

Of course, it is not just our inner noise that keeps us in Egypt, but our companions along the way, too. A chorus of voices from our friends and families and co-workers might also be trying to keep us where we are—in the world,

---

[32] 1 Kings 19:12

because if we changed, then they might have to change, too. The sense of betrayal is huge when we embark on a totally different path. We might lose friends or the goodwill of others when we listen to that "still, small voice." I finally realized that if I am true to myself and to God, while others might not like what I am proposing to do, eventually it works out for them, too; especially, in my case, my husband. I was modeling for him a new way of living; he might not like what I was going to do right then, but my being true to myself also gave him permission to be true to himself. And so, regardless of the flack I got, I would do what God was inspiring me to do. It was only after my surrender to God that I had the courage to follow that inner wisdom.

This is a crucifixion of sorts, a death to the old ways of doing things, of being enslaved to the culture, to an outer referencing for my life. I had to die to others' opinion of who I was and am, including what I should be doing in order to embrace my true self. As Fr. Richard Rohr puts it, "While resurrection is where incarnation leads, there is one caveat, and it's a big one: transformation and 'crucifixion' must intervene between life and Life. Some form of loss, metamorphosis or transformation always precedes any rejuvenation."[33]

Here is G____'s story of leaving all this behind: "When I decided to be baptized, I spoke to my heavenly Father and said, 'I will follow you. I will repent if I have sinned. I will spread Your Word as your Apostles did. I will serve the sick and feed those who I see hungry. I will follow the commandments of God. My body is your temple. I will receive the Holy Spirit. In turn I know you will bless me,

---

[33]Fr. Richard Rohr's Daily Email 1.22.16 *God's Solidarity with Suffering*

feed me, make sure I have a roof over my head. I know you will make sure I'm not alone. I will fear not, because you are always with me. You will heal me. I will always go to the house of the Lord. You have blessed me time and time again and there will be more blessings to come.' " This is a strong statement that she is leaving the cares of the world behind.

In religious terms incarnation means that the Indwelling Spirit of God has emerged from its potential within us, to leading us in all we do. That is the product of God's transforming us into the people He created us to be after our "crucifixion" or death to the world. This is what Jesus modeled for us--after His death in the world, by the world, He was resurrected.

Suffering calls us to suffer—quickest way through the pain

If we only knew that the way out of suffering is to suffer, to feel the pain, to allow our grief to flow, that shame would to rise to the surface for what we've done or what was done to us, so that we could be healed. If we can face our suffering head on, then it no longer enslaves us, ties us to the past. If you've ever known someone who has been abused as a child, either sexually or verbally, it takes a long time as adults, sometimes decades of work, to get past that experience. But s/he can come out on the other side to a place of being a valuable person in his/her own right instead of being ashamed of who they are or what was done to them (as if it was somehow their fault!). When we are a captive of our pain, we suffer immeasurably. It defines us, tells us how unworthy we are. And it keeps us tied to our past. The same is true of unexpressed grief from the loss of a parent or friend, spouse or close relative; it ties us to the past and means we cannot move on to a new life without thoroughly grieving that person.

Our willingness to be enslaved to the past means that we are running away from something, usually something that we can't bear to face. We have opted out of facing head on what we did or what was done to us and become addicted to some substance or alcohol or we choose an activity that will help us forget the pain--we could go shopping, keep ourselves too busy to look at it, bury our nose in a book or play endless video games and more--these are all addictions when we use them to escape the pain we've suffered. Even the extreme busyness of today, working long hours, going home to children with their needs, and spouses with theirs, we are overworking and unable to enjoy the downtime, because we cannot actually relax and just be. This is slavery, as is the notion that we have no choice, but to do this.

When we experience the grief and guilt and shame in ourselves fully, we can let it go. We can move out of our slavery to it, to keeping it hidden, to keep God and others from judging us. The suffering in our childhood particularly formed a lot of our reactions to the world and our enslavement to its values. But when we decide to leave the past behind us, to leave our enslavement to it, we are no longer ruled by the pain. We can see ourselves as valued, even loved and forgiven by God.

Part I: Awakening

Chapter Five

Conclusions

Conclusion: Escaping the grip of slavery

There are lots of ways to leave Egypt, both voluntarily and without a choice. There is a sense of relief at first in just being free of the Egyptians, if we leave voluntarily. If we were thrown out of Egypt, say by grief or a storm or illness or job loss, it may take longer before we can see some benefit in where we've landed.

We and the Israelites escape from slavery!!! And yet, the hold it has on us does not disappear just because we got away! The Egyptian army chasing after us with the Pharaoh leading the charge means that we still have the mindset of the captive; we are still liable to harassment and to being caught again in slavery's traps. This is Part I of the story. We have left Egypt and with God's grace are physically free of the Egyptians, but that is not the end of the story. As Parts II and III tell it, we are still captivated by the thought of returning to Egypt, still attached to being slaves in "Egypt." It remains our "home," our normal. We forget all the problems there and retain only fond memories of it. We remember all our needs being taken care of there and forget all about the abuse we suffered.

The Lord instructed Moses when the Egyptians were in sight to move his staff over the waters of the Sea of Reeds; Moses turned it into dry land. The Israelites were about half-way across when the Egyptians entered the sea, and had reached the other side when Moses again waved his staff over the dry pathway and commanded the waters to return, drowning all the Egyptians.

Baptism by water—Red Sea

The Sea of Reeds or the Red Sea is the first barrier we cross on this journey led by God. It is a baptism by water, a symbolic crossing from the world into God's care; now God's children, we follow Him where He would take us. Later, as we cross the River Jordan, we will experience a baptism of the Spirit. But for now, we have left Egypt. Of course, Egypt's powers-that-be are chasing us, but they are all caught in the return of the waters, while we have escaped. We're on the other side!! Safe and free, or so we think.

Baptism by water is all about identification with God, faith and obedience. We have left Egypt. We're on the other side!! We're following God! We can relax, at least for now!

And we, like the Israelites, will sing a song of praise to God for freeing us from slavery.

"I will sing to the Lord,

for he is highly exalted.

Both horse and driver

He has hurled into the sea.

The Lord is my strength and my defense;

he has become my salvation.

He is my God, and I will praise him,

My father's God, and I will exalt him."[34]

This is Miriam's song. There is the relief of escaping the Egyptian army, there is joy at being safe, there is celebration at the strength of the Lord. This is the first moment out of Egypt and we are celebrating. The next moment belongs to Part II.

The Exodus story, beginning with the Israelites being led out of Egypt by Moses, is the template that God has given us for how we go from slavery to the world into freedom. He calls an inner Moses to be his spokesman; I believe this is our soul stepping forward, now that we are

---

[34]Exodus 15:1-2

paying attention to it, so that it can lead us out of our oppression. As long as we are enslaved to the world, the soul, the shy, retiring soul, remains inactive in us. But with this call from God for us to get ready to leave Egypt, we are dependent on the soul to hear Moses' voice; we are dependent on God for how to extricate ourselves. And God, through Moses, does some pretty impressive tricks before Pharaoh to impress on him the need to let us go. And so, the soul has already come forward in our lives to begin to take its place at our center.

Look to Part II for the second part of our journey in God....

Lessons from Part I

1) It is difficult to leave Egypt. No matter how flawed and difficult life for us is there, it is our home and we like the familiar. We have become comfortable over time with the loss of our freedom. We know the territory. And wasn't that how exactly Pharaoh enslaved us?

It is enormously difficult for us to leave the world, the Pharaoh and Egypt itself, because we can't imagine living any other way. It is often because we won't feel our pain and suffering, hiding it from ourselves, from others and from God that causes the difficulty. Until we can bear the pain, face it head on, and grieve for it, we will stay enslaved to it.

2) God is in charge of our leaving and in charge of the factors that keep the Israelites bound to Egypt. He wants to lead us to freedom from slavery, but He does it, as the conditions are ripe, with the most chance of success.

3) Entrenched interests never want to let go. Successive plagues finally loosen Pharaoh's grip; the deaths of the firstborn children and livestock convince him. And even then, after the Israelites are gone, he heads out after them to bring them back. It takes a long time in the wilderness before this inner power struggle ceases—40 days plus 40 years before the draw of the Pharaoh/ego within has no more power over us. It's not that the ego is destroyed; it's that it no longer functions on its own. It will be brought under the aegis of the soul.

4) For us, the Pharaoh's voice will be the one that clings to the known, that fears the unknown, that wants to rule us. Our willingness to be enslaved means that we are running away from something, usually some great suffering, pain, sorrow or just our own self-image in the culture that we can't bear to face.

5) God is always calling us out of slavery, sowing the seeds of freedom, dropping hints in our minds that would show us the way out.

And so goes our enslavement to anything of this world. It takes a long time to get over being a captive of what enslaves us. We've just taken the first step out of slavery, but we'll find that its effects last a long time. To be willing to leave our enslavement, we have to disengage from the old, the past, to be in limbo for a while, until we can learn a new way of being, but that is the story of Part II.

In Part II we'll be looking at the next step, which is being in limbo in the wilderness, neither enslaved, but not yet free either....

*   *   *

Part II: The Wilderness

Chapter One

Introduction to the Wilderness

Part II covers Exodus Chapters 15 –34

Introduction

Part II of the Exodus story finds the Israelites in the wilderness wandering, seemingly with no clear direction. They have to depend on God, but they feel deserted in a wasteland. Here we experience real spiritual desolation. We feel abandoned by friends, spouse, and God, even as He is clearly visible. Every hope evaporates the moment we reach for it. Every dream dies the moment we try to realize it. We question, we doubt, we struggle. Nothing helps. We pray and the words seem empty. We turn to the Bible and find it meaningless. We turn to music and it fails to move us, unless maybe it's a requiem. We seek the fellowship of other

Christians and discover only backbiting, selfishness and egoism. The Biblical metaphor for these experiences of forsakenness is the desert or wilderness. It is an apt image, for we do indeed feel dry, barren, and parched. With the Psalmist we cry out, "My God, I cry out day by day, but you do not answer."[36] In fact, we begin to wonder if there is a God to answer.

My friend, Matt, who is a street preacher, told me recently, "I did everything I was supposed to do [for God]." And he ended up homeless. His statement comes from the first stage of the wilderness. We are following the laws, doing everything we've been taught about what pleases God, we think, but we don't necessarily have a relationship with God, we are not being led by God, we are just trying to be obedient to the laws. This is letter-of-the-law obedience, the first stage of the wilderness. It's the place of departure into a new life; first we have to go through the wilderness, where we launch a new identity in God when we have left the world.

This first part of the wilderness is the 2nd stage of the classic spiritual journey: *purgation*. It is a time of seeing ourselves without the usual cultural overlays, to see ourselves naked and defenseless. As we experience the wilderness and all the uncertainty and vulnerability that it brings, we are undone. The wilderness is a dangerous place where we are without defenses. But then there is God visible to us all the time: "By day the Lord went ahead of them in a pillar of cloud to guide them on their way and by night in a pillar of fire to give them light, so that they could travel by day or night. Neither the pillar of cloud by day nor the pillar

---

[36] Psalm 22:2

of fire by night left its place in front of the people."[37] God is the blessing of the wilderness. It is God who has led us there and who will be with us the whole time.

But it is the wilderness that is the most important character of this part of the story. It's a no-where place filled with dangers and little to recommend it. It's an out-of-time place, too. Days drag on, nights might be barren of sleep, as I recently experienced. Then everything is colored by the lack of sleep and the drag it causes on your days.

I have divided the forty years in the wilderness into two parts. Part II of this book deals with the obvious "sinfulness" of God's people, the conscious acts of disobedience to God. It ends after the Israelites chose to worship Baal, the second tablets of the Ten Commandments are given to the Israelites by Moses, and the Tent of Meeting is set up. In Part III the wilderness stay is about the deeper obedience to God—the giving up of the unconscious rebellion/attachment to the world's ways. The second stage of the spiritual journey, *Purgation,* continues the catharsis, purification and refining in the longer wilderness stay, but then leads to *Illumination* when a person is able to worship God with all of himself, to be obedient in all His ways, to be in partnership with God in fulfilling His purpose.

Wilderness

The wilderness is an in-between place. It is not Egypt or the world, nor is it the Promised Land. It is a becoming, reorienting place. It's where we shed the old and learn how to live in the new reality that is before us. It is a place of

---

[37] Exodus 13:21-22

limbo where big decisions are postponed until we're clear about where we're going and how we will get there, that includes vision of what our lives will be like. It's a place where we are off-balance and vulnerable. And interestingly, it is a place where God is very visible. And in our vulnerability we have a great need for God.

His visible presence was a source of great comfort, I am sure, for the Israelites, but it hardly calmed their fears. Everything was new and uncomfortable. There seemed to be no safety. And quickly they found their needs not being met.

Here's the story of the wilderness by one of my readers, A_____: "The very thing I resented the most I became...that was my wilderness experience, and that's not the half of it. As a result of myself-run-riot, I lost my children, 2 beautiful babies... which you'd think would cause me to stop, but 'it took what it took' to bring me to my level of spiritual bankruptcy. And that is when I could no longer look at myself. Several things brought me to the end of myself, and I found the solution: Admitting Complete Defeat. I surrendered my will over to the care of God 20 years ago, and I have not been the same [since]."

She continues, "God delivered me from all roots of bitterness, animosity, regret, fear, feelings of rejection, and disappointments and lack of leadership that I had carried around in my heart against my Dad. My Dad and I regained a healthy relationship for ten of those years before the Lord called him home." Facing oneself—the "good, the bad and the ugly" as the old Western movie title put it, is a beginning. But it can't happen until we have left the old life.

In limbo, in the wilderness is where we thoroughly grieve any losses we have suffered. Until we can fully grieve our losses, we will be living in the past. We will long to be back in that place that was so problematic for us. We will long to go back and reclaim our old lives, anything to get out of the wilderness.

Being in limbo may come into your life, as it did into my husband's and mine when both of our twins were in the hospital, then six weeks old. One was in a respirator tent with bronchitis and the other on a respirator, so overcome by pneumonia that he had stopped breathing at home. For seven seemingly endless days we didn't know if the second twin would survive.

During that week we could not make any decisions at all, except to spend as much time at the hospital as we could. Our lives were suspended, in limbo, until we knew if he'd live or die. Nothing was important to us, except his life. Fortunately, he did survive, but we were changed by the prospect of losing him. Nothing that we had thought important mattered at all, while we waited for the outcome of the disease, especially not the material things.

Even after we knew he would be fine, we reacted to every cough and odd thing as if he would die again. We called one pediatrician on call so many times, especially in the middle of the night. As we finally settled down, we called that pediatrician at 8 o'clock one evening with a question. He asked us why we were calling so early, it wasn't even midnight yet!

The desert may come with the loss of a job or the death of a parent or a Tsunami or any catastrophic event in our lives. Or we may choose to follow the leadings of the Lord and walk into the wilderness, leaving our attachments to slavery behind. Whatever the cause that puts us in the wilderness, we have to get to know the territory and see what God is asking of us.

It may come in an alcoholic treatment center. Hear B_____ and her story. "I am a recovering alcoholic. I am a child of God, 51 years old, a mother of 3, grandmother of 2, one on the way. I am employed at a drug and alcohol recovery center, three years now. God brought me here at the age of 47. I was broken in every way possible. I had been in active addiction in and out for 22 years. It was here I learned I had a disease. It was here I learned [what] God could and would do if He were sought. I surrendered fully to His will."

In the desert nothing is familiar and everything seems worth complaining about. Water is hard to find in the wilderness. And did the Israelites complain about that! God had Moses strike a rock at Horeb and the water flowed.[38] Water represents many things in the Bible, but most importantly it represents the Word of God. The Gospel is a cleansing agent and the source of living water; anyone who drinks of this water will never thirst.[39] In an echo of purgation, cleansing bubbles up in the water. The Lord is meeting our physical needs with the basic source of all life, water, and our spiritual needs with the transformative Word of God.

---

[38] Exodus 17:6

[39] http://www.patheos.com/blogs/christiancrier/2015/07/17/what-does-water-represent-in-the-bible-a-christian-study/ John 4:14 9.17.16

The Israelites also complained about the lack of food, too, and the Lord produced manna every morning for forty years.[40] It was unfamiliar, and unexciting food, but it was nutritious and present every morning. The only day they were allowed to stockpile manna was the day before the Sabbath; otherwise it would rot. And then God provided quail every evening.[41] So the Lord is meeting their needs and still the Israelites are complaining.

At Elim where the quail and manna were given, the Israelites found twelve wells of water and seventy palm trees, riches that would slake their thirst and provide shade and dates as well.[42] Elim provided a lush oasis in the middle of the desert for the Israelites, a respite.

It is easy to get discouraged when we are brought out of Egypt, but God has a plan for our next step. God will bring us out of slavery, even the slavery that remains in our habitual thinking. He will free us from both the physical situations and the accompanying thinking, but for our part we have to be open to where God is leading us, to the journey along the way, even as God is working inside us, too, healing and transforming and lessening our attachment to our story and to the ways of the world.

Only God can fill what we hunger and thirst for. In the Exodus story, what the Israelites want is food and water, especially food that is familiar to them. What do we hunger and thirst for? Ultimately, once our physical needs are met, we long to be at home in our lives, to feel at peace; we long

---

[40] Exodus 16:35
[41] Exodus 16:13
[42] Exodus 15:27

to be in communion with our Source; we also long to have integrity and to fulfill our purpose on this Earth. The answer to all this longing is God, who is also longing for us to return to Him.[43] He will free us of all our ties to the world's ways, if we are willing to follow His lead.

It is the nature of people in the wilderness to not trust, to complain, to feel unsettled, to wish we were back in the familiar, even if the familiar was a form of slavery. The first part of the *Purgation* stage of the spiritual journey, the outer conformity to God's Laws, is the part of the Exodus story, from the Red Sea to Mount Sinai. They stayed there for quite a while allowing Moses to spend 40 days twice up on Mount Sinai with the Lord. I would set the end of this part of the wilderness story when Moses sets up the Tent of Meeting,[44] after the debacle with Ba'al, after the second of Moses' long stays on the mountain with God, when the Law of the Ten Commandments was given to the Israelites the second time.

Egypt represents hardness of heart, imprisonment of body and mind, punishment of the body in brutal work, all conditions that beat down the human spirit, in which no one thrives, only survives, if that. It's no wonder that we want to get as far away as possible from the slavery, that we will follow God into a new place. And yet, we are torn between going and staying, between a new life and old certainties. Is that why some criminals when released commit a crime right away so as to reenter the very prison they just left? Or why the abused spouse stays with her abuser? Isn't the familiar more comfortable than the unknown??

---

[43] Luke 15:11ff The Parable of the Lost Son
[44] Exodus 33:7-11

I____, another reader, was an abused wife who sought God's help in changing her violent husband, but He never did. Finally, after 12 years, the police transported her to a battered women's shelter, her faith in God gone. Addiction to alcohol and methamphetamines followed. Through the prayers of her family and God's grace she quit after 3 years, then relapsed and almost died. She has now married a good man; both of them asked God back into their lives. Now eight years later, "God rules and reigns and is the Lord and Savior of our lives!" The wilderness lies between the decision to leave the world of addiction behind and the true capitulation of our lives to God.

God brought the Israelites out of Egypt, yet, in the wilderness, the Israelites were wishing they were back in Egypt. They had not left Egypt behind in their minds, even though the experience there was horrific. In the forty days of wandering in the desert and the eighty days[45] at the foot of Mount Sinai there was too much uncertainty, with a seemingly remote God, as Moses spent 40 days up on the mountain twice. Egypt represented the known, the normal, so the pain of slavery there was forgotten.

We, too, need to be brought out of slavery today, out of our narrow ways of thinking and ideas that no longer work for us that we absorbed from others and from our culture, so that we, too, can live in the present. Even if we haven't suffered from any addictions or haven't lost a loved one, even if we have a great life, we still long to live an integrated and whole life. We are still enslaved to the culture. It's hard to leave behind what is so familiar to us and to launch out into the unknown. What will be our

---

[45] approximately

identity if we give up our story? Will we find our footing? Will we lose our way? Can we run back to the familiar and take comfort in its old, worn security blanket? For everyone transitions are not fun, much less a forty-year transition in the wilderness.

Here's how my reader C_____ weathered the wilderness: "During my storm I was in the wilderness for 9 years. God spoke to me and he said these words: 'before your journey is over you will know who I am,' just as He had spoken to Moses. People on my job treated me very badly and for 9 years God told me to stand [to stay]. In those 9 years of being in the wilderness, the adversaries could not make any of their allegations stick. His Word was and is my manna. The blood of Jesus Christ will never lose its power. He protected me for 9 years. I wish I could tell you the whole story."

It is hard to remember that our needs are being met in the move to a not-yet-realized place, to remember that God is present with us in the current difficulties. Having moved out of the familiar into the unknown seems risky at best and more frightening as time goes on, with the new life not yet here and the old life too far off to return to.

The inner landscape we are traveling in this early part of the wilderness is the outward adherence to the laws of God. Remember that God is trying to take us to the Promised Land, to the Kingdom; the first step is conformity to the Laws of God, particularly the Ten Commandments. It is God working on the outer, visible aspects of ourselves here in the first part of the wilderness story.

This first part of the wilderness experience is mercifully short, a few months. The task here is to orient our outer selves to God. It is the second stage of the big transition from the world to the Kingdom. But it is essential to tackle these visible rebellions towards God before we start working on the unconscious ones. The wilderness is stark and forbidding, in contrast to our memories of the place we left, which are much more positive than they actually were.

The wilderness is an in-between place, a not-yet place. We might still be sick. We might still not have a job after losing one. We might be in temporary housing. We may just be in an inner wilderness where nothing is the same as what we are used to. We are in limbo, neither in Egypt nor in the Promised Land. Nothing within us has changed so far, only the circumstances we find ourselves in.

Several years ago, I moved three times in a year and a half. First, I followed my daughter and son-in-law and their family to Baltimore from Charlotte. His job there didn't work out, so at the end of the school year we moved back to Charlotte. I rented an apartment for six months in Charlotte while I looked for a permanent place to live. Then I moved into a townhome. Much in me was shaken loose in all these moves—old habits, ways of thinking, attachments, but the major way it left me feeling was that there was no ground on which to put my feet. I was rootless. Finally, almost a year after I moved the last time, I felt that I had a "home," a place to put my feet. This was a wilderness experience for me. Interestingly, at the same time I am experiencing all that dislocation, I had never felt more tightly held by God.

As Robert Mulholland writes in *Invitation to a Journey*, "What we don't realize is that often a period of apparent spiritual stagnation, a time in which we don't feel as if we are going anywhere, a phase of life in which our relationship with God seems weak or nonexistent, the time of dryness, of darkness…is filled with nurturing down below the surface that we never see."[46]

On the surface we are experiencing a lack of nourishment, food and water. We are worried and missing our home, no matter how problematic it was. At least it was intimately known to us. Here in the wilderness, everything is unfamiliar. We may have physically left the world, but we are still attached to its ways of thinking and seeing. We miss everything about Egypt!

The wilderness is a place where we relinquish all our old ways, habits of thinking, attachments to the way we like things to be, guilt and shame, and attachments to people or things that come between us and God. We are neither here, nor there. Our footing in the world is questionable in this dangerous place.

In the wilderness we grumble and complain a lot. We are torn between what we hope for ourselves—an end to slavery—and a fear that we have gone about it in the wrong way. There is little trust of God at this point. And yet, God is still our reason for living, the ground under our feet. It's just that our ego is so disrupted.

Grief is also an issue. In leaving the world we are experiencing our attachments to the way things were. The past, however problematic, looks much better than the

---

[46] L. Robert Mulholland, *Invitation to at Journey: A Road Map for Spiritual Formation*, IVP Books, Downers Grove IL, 1993, p. 21

present. So, we long to return. There is a lot to grieve, not just what we have lost, but the terror of a journey through an unknown land where we have no control over anything. We are tempted, as Jesus was tempted in the wilderness,[47] by the ways of the world. They loom large and wonderful in our imagination and memories as we contemplate an uncertain future.

Hear how a young grieving widow, A____, is coping with her loss: "My husband just passed away and we are young. We had a whole life ahead of us. Not just high school sweethearts but elementary school sweethearts. I've questioned God, I've questioned my own faith and I've trusted God. It's by far the worst experience of my entire 31 years. But then there's God. He's giving me so much strength. Strength that, I myself, am amazed at. A strength I cannot put into words. We have four babies; I'm working two jobs. Some days I don't know how I'm going to do it...And those days pass. It's been almost four weeks. I'm not sure what's ahead, but I'm just taking it day by day." All that pain and there is God helping her through it.

We also need to grieve all the pain and suffering we have been through, the pain we have caused others. Until these incidences are grieved thoroughly, we will stay anchored in the past, unable to be present to where God is taking us and to what He wants us to learn. Forgiveness is important, too. We need to forgive ourselves for all that we have said and done and to forgive those who have hurt us. If we don't forgive, again, we are not able to leave the past behind. We'll be nurturing our wounds and not listening to what God has in store for us.

---

[47] Matthew 4:1-11

It is another challenge to be so totally dependent on God, having to consult with Him about the least decisions. It is the time of giving up our expectations, assumptions and preferences—all the things which the ego promotes. As Sue Monk Kidd writes, "In touch with my neediness, I came face to face with my dependence on God—not only for my future but for my next breath. What can we do but acknowledge that dependence and trust God? In this posture of owning our weakness, we're transformed. For that's how the soul is born and reborn: as we quit servicing the ego and acknowledge our weaknesses. Strength in weakness is the paradox of the cocoon."[48]

In the wilderness as we let go of the past, we are learning to live in the present: first, to be aware of dangers around us; secondly, to see our own interior state of being clearly: thirdly, to be able to see where God is, that He is with us every step of the journey. We have to learn to set aside how we've always thought in favor of living in God's presence, thinking like God thinks, depending on Him without question. And also, we must accept the reality that we have to deal with, instead of wishing we were back in Egypt. As the Mulholland quote above puts it, "our relationship with God seems weak or non-existent."[49] That's because we have not moved into an inner relationship with Him yet, a partnership. In this first step we are still looking at God as an outer authority.

As a first step on this journey in how to live in the Promised Land, the Kingdom, Moses' father-in-law, Jethro, comes to visit—insists that Moses needs help in adjudicating

---

[48] Sue Monk Kidd, *When the Heart Waits*, p. 142
[49] Mulholland, p. 21

all the issues among the people. He suggests that Moses appoint judges to serve under him to help judge the lesser issues, leaving Moses free to take on the tougher ones.[50] This is the first step in reorganizing how he and the Israelite community were to live. Much more detailed reorganizations were a part of the Mosaic laws handed down before and after the debacle of Ba'al.

This first phase of the wilderness journey is about surrendering to the laws, particularly the Ten Commandments. More on this in the next chapter.

---

[50]Exodus 18:1ff

Part II: The Wilderness

Chapter Two

God, Laws, Moses

Where God is Visible, Omnipresent

The wilderness is a place where God is very visible to us. It is in our suffering that God is most visible; we can often sense His presence in our pain. When things are going well for us, we may hardly notice God; we really don't need Him, we think.

Chris Webb writes beautifully in *The Fire of the Word* about how God works. Pay close attention to these words: "This act of liberation was pure gift, pure grace. God called his people, God redeemed them, God set them free, God preserved them at the Red Sea, God sustained them in the wilderness—without any 'Law.' Grace, as always, came first.

This is the nature of God."[51] First, grace is extended; then come the laws that God would have us follow. And later still, in the second phase of the wilderness, the laws get more detailed and complex and we must be obedient in our minds and hearts and souls and bodies as well as in our conscious and unconscious thinking. Our purpose gets spelled out. This is the process that prepares us to live in the Promised Land, in the Kingdom of God."

Not only has God led us out of slavery, but in the wilderness God is in charge of the direction we travel, the experiences we have and the challenges we face. The wilderness is the place where our attachments and everything that would keep us from God are highlighted and need to be let go of.

At this point in the journey God is dealing with a fairly fractious individual or group who is only beginning to learn to trust. And so a good part of the first part of the wilderness is learning to begin to trust that God will answer our needs. That He will answer our prayers, although not always in the form that we requested.

Listen to how one reader of mine, D_____, has described the desert experience: "Every tunnel between one closed door and a new open window has been a prayer closet. At first it feels dark, lonely and scary...but as I cried out for relief Jesus didn't always change my circumstance or my abilities. He showed up and sat in the dark with me until the atmosphere of my circumstance was filled with His Love. Comfort and death defying Strength. He became the

---

[51] Chris Webb, *The Fire of the Word: Meeting God on Holy Ground*, IVP Books, Downers Grove, IL, 2011, p. 54

door, the tunnel, the closet, the window. He became everything to me and therefore I discovered salvation is in HIM, not only in His immediately delivering me from earthly woes. Hallelujah! I love Jesus!"

Her use of the word tunnel to describe the wilderness reflects on the space, the time, between leaving the world and entering the Promised Land. The tunnel again is a place of darkness and unknown destination. It suggests the in-between place where we discover who we really are, all in the presence of God.

Another reader, R_____, lost her daughter five years ago and is raising her two grandsons. It is hard, but she has seen many break-throughs and many blessings. "But I think the tunnel will continue until these boys are raised. One is headed for technical school in the fall." This is yet another example of how the transition between the world and God feels when we are dealing with difficult circumstances. And of how it can be a long time between when her daughter died and she finishes raising her grandsons—time in the wilderness.

The Israelites grumbled a lot to Moses about the lack of good water or food: "If only we had died by the Lord's hand in Egypt! There we sat around pots of meat and ate all the food we wanted, but you have brought us out into this desert to starve this entire assembly to death."[52] I think it is interesting that God didn't just provide their needs. Certainly He knew them, but waited for the Israelites to articulate them. We have to bring our needs to God, too, in

---

[52] Exodus 16:3

prayer. It's important for us to be aware of all the aspects of our inner states of being.

As with their complaints about water, which God delivered plentifully to them at site after site, God provided manna for the Israelites every day for over forty years![53] In the wilderness God is providing all our needs as we ask for them. It is not just the physical needs that He is prepared to meet, but our spiritual needs, in addition to safety and protection from our enemies, too.

"As God closes one door there is a season of waiting, hoping, praying and sometimes doubting what God has done and what he's doing…In laying our doubts and fears at the Master's feet, peace and strength are given back to us [so] we can stand a little longer until God says, 'it's time, here's your door.'" Reader S____ continues: "He[Jesus] wraps His loving arms around us so we can hide and lean on Him and carries us sometimes especially when the door of promise has been closed longer than our personal time table, if we were to be real about it. But His grace is sufficient, if we pick it up and put it on."

Another reader, E____, had a recurring dream about doors which brought her comfort: "[In the dream] I lived in in a shack. I wasn't even unhappy in it, but one day I found a door and opened it. My Shack was connected to like a trailer house; I lived there and one day I opened a door and [there] was a three-bedroom brick home, then [another door] and a mansion. This dream always confused me. Because who lives in a home and doesn't know all the places in it? But in life there is always stuff that is right there if we just

---

[53] Exodus 16:35

look. [Occasionally,] I still have a similar dream and 'Lo and Behold!' there is another room, another set of furniture, a whole new kitchen…There will always be doors. I try to be happy where I am, but I think life is a series of doors!" God seems to be telling her that there is another way to look at things, a passage where we expect none, a "door" into a bigger reality, God's own reality.

God reminds the Israelites that He has brought them as far as the Desert of Sinai:"You yourselves have seen what I did to Egypt, and how I carried you on eagles' wings and brought you to myself. Now if you obey me fully and keep my covenant, then out of all nations you will be my treasured possession. Although the whole earth is mine, you will be for me a kingdom of priests and a holy nation."[54] And the Israelites agreed.

God here reminds the Israelites of all that He has done for them in freeing them from slavery. He iterates His covenant and the potential within the Israelites and the freedom to which He is calling them. God has to constantly remind us of His presence and aid in our lives, because we forget so easily and fall back on our own meager resources.

It is so interesting to me that from God's point of view, He brought us to the desert on eagles' wings. From our point of view we might have been dragged here kicking and screaming! Just an illustration of how differently we think from the way God thinks!

Another reader F____ has reported that she has been homeless since Katrina. She's lived in a FEMA tent city, then

---

[54] Exodus 19:4-6

a "FEMA-hell" trailer park and then a bed bug-infested retirement complex. She lost everything three times in 10 years and turned to addiction. When she complained to God, He told her that He was proud of how far she had come. But, she replied, "But losing everything 3X in 10 years?" "This time," He said, "It was my chance to do it faithfully and gracefully." "I've been in recovery five years now. He's still moving me around. Everywhere I go, I've had the opportunity to share my faith. I got to spend the last month as a live-in caretaker for a close friend of mine. What an honor to be placed in that home just in time to help P____ prepare to meet his Maker. We had plenty of time to share our faith. I have so many stories to tell about God's miraculous working in my life."

F____ has experienced what all of us who have experienced the wilderness know: that God has a greater, more interesting life in store for us, one in which we will serve God and other people with our gifts and talents and what we have learned from our own pain and suffering, now healed and redeemed.

As we people are inconstant, still God is there for us. He waits for us to return to Him as we see in the Parable of the Lost Son.[55] I think that we are surprised that He still wants us no matter what we have done. One woman, G____, was saved in 1983, but was inconstant in living her life for God. She chose the wrong men. She raised 4 children, sometimes in a 1 bedroom apartment; she was on and off welfare. Still God was helping her. Estranged friends would offer to help, one to take her youngest daughter to the bus stop every day for a summer; another offered to pay

---

[55] Luke 15:11ff

whatever bill was the hardest for her to pay until she got on her feet. In her own words, "Once God chooses you even if it takes a life time, He will get His glory out of you, keep the faith, stay a soldier for the Lord. He loves us and wants what's best for us. Trust Him. We may not be able to see Him, but we can see Him working in our lives; we can hear Him speak so softly and calmly, yet firmly."

I want to add here that I have never thought that God was surprised that we are an inconstant and difficult people. I don't think He was surprised at Adam and Eve taking a bite of the apple in the Garden of Eden. Let me lay out my reasoning for this. God designed and created this immense universe (and maybe multiple universes as the cosmologists now postulate), which is interdependent and productive for all life. On this Earth scientists think there are more than seven million species of plants and animals all in an interdependent system in which each species of plants and animals contributes to the life of others. For instance, there are probably more than 300,000 species of beetles on Earth. Now God either created one beetle with the capacity to morph into that many species depending on the conditions in which it dwells or He created that many species of beetles. And that is just one insect. I would argue that the mind of God that could create such detail and a whole interdependent system of life could not possibly be surprised that giving us free will would make us a petulant, inconstant people. He gave us free will. So apparently, He wants us to come of our own volition.

As loving as God can be, He can be overwhelming, too, for the Israelites. The Lord tells Moses that He will appear in a dense cloud at the foot of Mount Sinai, "so that the people will hear me speaking with you and will always put their trust in you."[56] So the people consecrated themselves for two days and were given further instructions on where they were to stand. On the third day "There was thunder and lightning, with a thick cloud over the mountain, and a very loud trumpet blast. Everyone in the camp trembled. Then Moses led the people out of the camp to meet with God, and they stood at the foot of the mountain. Mount Sinai was covered with smoke, because the Lord descended on it in fire. The smoke billowed up from it like smoke from a furnace, and the whole mountain trembled violently."[57]

The Lord spoke the Ten Commandments to Moses. The people "trembled with fear" and asked Moses to be God's spokesperson, "but do not have God speak to us or we will die."[58]

God in this first part of the wilderness story will not be approached directly, even though He is highly visible everywhere they go. He is so fearsome to the Israelites that they prefer an intermediary between them and God. They will not approach Him directly, but they will try their best to obey His laws.

The 10 Commandments

At Mount Sinai God handed down the Ten Commandments verbally, first to the assembled Israelites, and then on tablets to Moses. The laws deal with how to love and worship God and how to treat your parents and

---

[56] Exodus 19:9
[57] Exodus 19:16-18
[58] Exodus 20:18-19

neighbors. These are the principles of the detailed laws He will hand down now and later in Exodus, Leviticus, Numbers and Deuteronomy. The first four commandments are about worshipping God: no other gods before me, no graven images, no misuse of the Lord's name, keeping the Sabbath day holy. God is clearly to be first in our lives and not taken for granted. The 5th Commandment is to honor your father and mother. The last five have to do with how we treat our neighbors. Do not murder, do not commit adultery, do not steal, do not give false testimony against your neighbor and do not covet anything that belongs to your neighbor. [59]

These principles are to guide our behavior in all that we do. 1) Keep God first in your life. 2) Honor your parents. 3) Treat your neighbors well. I maintain that if we keep the first four, if we're in the proper relationship with God, we cannot violate any of the other commandments. We literally could not do anything that would offend God. We could not abuse anyone of anything; we would, of course treat our parents well, as well as everyone else. Our needs will all be met by God, so we would have no need to treat anyone else badly. There would be no envy in us or competition or need to lie or to commit adultery.

Other Laws

While the Ten Commandments set out the principles of the law, the Lord went on to fill in the details as He continued talking to Moses on Mount Sinai. There were laws about how to treat Hebrew servants, men and women,[60] an

---

[59] Exodus 20:2-17
[60] Exodus 21:1-11

altar for burnt offerings,[61] personal injuries intentional and unintentional,[62] protection of property,[63] and social responsibility.[64] For example the laws about social responsibility included how to treat foreigners, what to do with those who sacrifice to other gods, with charging no interest if you lend to one of God's people and with prohibiting the blaspheming of God.

As we read through these laws we can see that they are the basis for many of our laws today. That's how far-reaching Mosaic Law has been. There are many laws that just wouldn't apply today, at least not in our non-agrarian societies, but of course the principles remain as a guide for us. There are also laws about worshipping God that don't apply, except to Orthodox Judaism today: the priestly garments and more.

Here is where we turn to Jesus' Two Great Commandments on which, in His words, "hang all the law and the prophets."[65] To love God with all of ourselves and to love our neighbor as ourselves—these two principles of the law, like the Ten Commandments, if followed, will stand us in good stead with the Lord. I repeat what I wrote before, if we follow the first four commandments, we cannot not treat our neighbors and our parents well, for they were created by the same God, as were we, in His image.[66]

---

[61] Exodus 20:24
[62] Exodus 21:12-35
[63] Exodus 22:1-15
[64] Exodus 22:16-31
[65] Matthew 22:36-40
[66] Genesis 1:26-27

In my own life since I was a teen-ager I had been passive aggressive towards my mother. "You can't make me do anything!" was what I tried to tell her over and over again, usually just in my mind. But there came a time after I surrendered my life to God when this question occurred to me: "How can I say I love God, if I can't even love my mother?" That confronted me where I was and started me on a journey with her that was difficult for me and probably for her, too. I tried to become an adult with her, but I was up against my training that said that I wasn't to talk back to my parents. So everything I said to her filled me with guilt as I disagreed with her or tried to engage her in a very different kind of dialogue.

This went on for a year or two, but we lived on opposite coasts, so we saw little of each other. Finally, Hank and I visited her one weekend in Wilmington, Delaware, where she lived, and as usual, I felt like a total bitch. She took us to the train station and stood with to us on the platform while we awaited the train. All I can say is that we were surrounded by a cloud of love. It lasted, oh, I don't know, maybe a few minutes. Then we said our goodbyes and got on the train.

All the way to Connecticut to see Hank's parents all I could say was, "I can't believe that God took my bitchiness and made it into love!" I was stunned. The amazing thing was that from that moment on, she was grateful for every single thing I ever did for her, instead of complaining about how I didn't write enough or call often enough or see her enough. And that cloud of love changed totally how I related to her. I could actually love her from then on. Later, after she had a stroke, she came to live ten minutes from us, where she really became a part of our family. We enjoyed her closeness the last four years of her life. God had healed all that rebellion in me towards her and healed her complaints about me.

The main principle we are to follow is to love God with everything we are. All else flows from that commandment. So, in any situation, the question is: *How would God want me to act now?* If we're in touch with God Himself, if we're in the *Illumination* stage of the wilderness, we'll hear it directly from God. If we're in the "Purgation" stage of the first part of the wilderness, then we may have to have detailed instructions from the Bible or someone to teach us how to be. For we will not have done the inner work on our attitudes and expectations, so that we can actually love another and God. If I hadn't been confronted by the question about loving God and my mother, I might have kept my attitude about her for the rest of my life. And what a waste that would have been-how much more guilt would have piled up within me?

No matter what the issue before us is, the question is always this: *If I love God, what do I need to do here?* In the rest of Exodus and in Leviticus, Numbers and Deuteronomy, God lays out detailed descriptions of how we are to act towards Him, towards our neighbors. If we are in the wilderness, we are learning how God wants us to behave, to be with Him, in great detail. We will always have this principle to act from, but God will also teach us how to react to every situation we confront. As He highlights our sins and unconscious attitudes in the wilderness, He will expect us to bring them to consciousness, admit that they are ours and, like the Israelites with Baal, we are to own up to all that we have done—to "drink" the remnants of the other gods.[67]

It is only when we have accepted responsibility for our behavior, forgiven ourselves for being human beings, and forgiven all that was done to us, that we are able with God to build a new attitude that shows His love. If we don't accept that we stray, that we make mistakes, then we have no chance of building a close relationship with the One who already knows all that we are. We're still trying to hide the worst that we've done, to deflect criticism, to not take responsibility. When we can't forgive another for any abuse we suffered, how can God work with that?

For right now, in the purgation stage of the journey, we are to align ourselves with God's Law, to begin to put Him first, to allow Him into at least the surface of our lives. Later, He will ask to go a lot deeper with us. But that is in Part III.

Moses

Moses continued as God's spokesperson from the Red Sea to Mount Sinai, in fact, all the way to the West Bank of the River Jordan. So far he has been a faithful and obedient servant of God. He is the go-between with God and the Israelites. He passes on all that God wants them to hear. He is the model of what a servant of God does.

As our inner "Moses," our soul is also where God speaks to us, where we can hear the "still, small voice of God,"[68] where we learn obedience to what He is telling us to

---

[67] Exodus 32:19-20
[68] 1 Kings 19:12 KJV

say or do or to be. As we develop that "inner ear," we hear God's voice more and more. We go from knowing God's Laws by heart to listening for God's voice in all things, from outward adherence to the Ten Commandments, to an inner attitude of putting God first in everything, to listening first of all to God, to being the servant of God that the Biblical Moses modeled for us. This is the task of the wilderness, but for now we're still in the first part of the wilderness, where the issue is our conformity to the laws as seen on the surface of our lives.

As we are converted from the ways of the world, our inner "Moses" comes forward in us, exerting more and more influence. He is how we communicate with God, especially how we hear God's voice, the voice of his "Indwelling Spirit." The more we are willing with our minds to give up the world's ways, the more we will conform to God's ways. As we give the soul and the Holy Spirit more space and play in our personalities, the ego gradually comes under the aegis of the soul. We don't have to become super-human or get rid of all our humanness, we just have to invest our humanity in the cause of the Divine.

There was a visible change in Moses as he again returned with the tablets of the Ten Commandments the second time. "He was not aware that his face was radiant because he had spoken with the Lord. When Aaron and all the Israelites saw Moses, his face was radiant, and they were afraid to come near him." Later he wore a veil over his face so it wouldn't disturb his countrymen. He would remove it only when he entered the Lord's presence in the tent of meeting.[69]

When the Israelites were attacked by the Amalekites at Rephidim, Moses told Joshua to choose some men and to fight them. Moses was to hold the staff of God in his hands. As long as his hands were held up, the Israelites were winning; when his arms were tired, they were losing. So they developed this strategy: when he got tired, he sat on a rock and Aaron and Hur held up his hands. So the Israelites defeated the Amalekites.[70]

Tent of Meeting

After Moses came down with the tablets a second time, he established a pattern of listening to God outside the Israelites' camp. "Now Moses used to take a tent and pitch it outside the camp some distance away, calling it the 'tent of meeting.' Anyone inquiring of the LORD would go to the tent of meeting outside the camp. And whenever Moses went out to the tent, all the people rose and stood at the entrances to their own tents, watching Moses until he entered the tent. As Moses went into the tent, the pillar of cloud would come down and stay at the entrance, while the LORD spoke with Moses. Whenever the people saw the pillar of cloud standing at the entrance to the tent, they all stood and worshiped, each at the entrance to their tent. The LORD would speak to Moses face to face, as one speaks to a friend. Then Moses would return to the camp,

---

[69] Exodus 34:29-35
[70] Exodus 17:8-16

but his young aide Joshua son of Nun did not leave the tent."[71]

Moses regularly spoke with God who appeared in a pillar of cloud. The people would worship at the entrance to their own tents while he spoke with God. Thus, the people established a reverence and worship of God. Moses remained God's spokesperson to his people.

---

[71] Exodus 33:7-11

Part II: The Wilderness

Chapter Three

Israelites, Conclusions

The Israelites are a "stiff-necked" people

After the Israelites crossed the Red Sea, they complained to Moses: "Was it because there were no graves in Egypt that you brought us to the desert to die? What have you done to us by bringing us out of Egypt?"[72] When they arrived at Marah, ". . . they could not drink its water because it was bitter…So the people grumbled against Moses, saying, 'What are we to drink.'"[73] They complained about the lack of food.[74] And again about being thirsty.[75]

Fear is the emotion the Israelites had to deal with all the time. One of my readers, H_____, writes what she has

---

[72] Exodus 14:11
[73] Exodus 15:23-4
[74] Exodus 16:1-4
[75] Exodus 17:1-3

been sensing: "The false reality we find ourselves in—FEAR or False Evidence Appearing Real, and the way we become conditioned to believe 'this is all there is.' What a lie!! The things we see have been created by an unseen God who has overcome all the trials we encounter. There's more to life than what we see." It will take the Israelites many years to learn this lesson.

As Moses is up on Mount Sinai with God for forty days receiving the Ten Commandments, the Israelites grow rebellious and frightened again. It's not the first time that they wished they could go back to Egypt! They persuade Aaron to help them build an idol, Ba'al, who they hope will lead them back to Egypt. They are scared of God whose voice they heard in the smoke at Mount Sinai, fearful of what has happened to Moses in all the days he had been gone and of what might happen to themselves. They turn their backs on God. And we do, too. We are inconstant, unable to resist the pulls of the world. So we turn our backs on God and then, if we admit to ourselves what we are doing, we turn back to God. Again and again.

In the wilderness we can experience two things at once if we are aware of God's presence in our lives. In one of my blog posts I said this after moving three times in two years: "A lot has been shaken loose in me, but I have been feeling like I have no solid ground beneath my feet. And at the same time I feel totally held by God. Now there is a paradox! A reader, I____, responded to this post: "How could you know without knowing what I have felt was sheer craziness going on with me and yet this morning the answer comes by way of your post. My throat has this huge lump in it and I feel like I cannot breathe...yet it is one of the most freeing moments I've felt in a long while."

Another reader, J____, wrote that God told her that the [several] moves were "just 'time off' to see and hear what the Lord wanted removed, pruned and grown." Another reason to be in the wilderness. What we with our world-view lenses see are problems and difficulties, but if we look for a deeper meaning in what is happening, we find a different reality. God is calling us to let go of something that is getting between us and God. It is all in how we look at things.

God with Moses up on the mountain tells Moses that the Israelites are building Ba'al. In anger he calls them a "stiff-necked people." [76]

Moses, as he came down the mountain with the two tablets in his hand, saw what the Israelites had done. He smashed the tablets, ruined the statue of Baal, reduced it to a liquid and made the Israelites drink it—metaphorically making them own what they had done. Then he went back up the mountain for another forty days so that God could remake the tablets.

God was furious at the "stiff-necked"[77] Israelites and wanted to destroy them. But Moses persuaded Him that He was forgetting His covenant with Abraham and that neighboring countries like Egypt will judge Him for helping

---

[76] Exodus 32:9
[77] Ibid

His people escape oppression only to kill them in the mountains.[78]

The Israelites represent us in the Exodus story; we are unable to consistently follow God's wishes for us, so we fall back on the world's ways. We are inconstant, unreliable and, yes, faithful, if we take going back into relationship after any serious misstep with God.

It is at this point in the story that the Ten Commandments are smashed by Moses and he goes back up to the mountain to commune with God another forty days. He finally comes back with the tablets, the rebellion is over, the law becomes the organizing principle of the wilderness journey.

Conclusion: Task of Part II of the Exodus Story

Like the Israelites we must give up our obvious rebelliousness and follow the laws in the Ten Commandments. We must own our mistakes, our sin. In this part of the wilderness, we are mainly dealing in the broad aspects of the Law. In the Exodus story 3,000 people are slain because of their rebellion in choosing to worship Baal instead of God.[79] I think that we have to take that metaphorically, that the parts of ourselves that are rebellious have to go, or come into alignment with our love of God, so that we can be more obedient. In fact, the whole wilderness journey of the Exodus story is about getting rid of all rebellion against God within us, but more about that later.

---

[78] Exodus 32:11-14
[79] Exodus 32:28

The difficulty we are faced with after we are freed from subservience, or any other painful condition, is that we keep it alive by telling and retelling our story. How wonderful it was in Egypt, all that great food, etc.! How hard it was, how awful those "Egyptians" [read parents, nuns, teachers, peers, bosses whoever held us in slavery to certain ideas whether they were true or not] were to us; any story has been a life long saga is perpetuated by all the retellings and we form great, bonded communities by everyone telling and retelling "our" stories. Or sometimes we are so ashamed of our story that we don't confide in anyone and still we hang onto it. The result is the same: We're tied to the past and unable to move on from it into a new life designed especially for us by God.

The question for us becomes this: Will we give up our grief and rebelliousness, so that we can obey God in all things? So that we can be present with Him in our lives? In the Hebrew language there are three main words that are translated "obey" in the Old Testament. The first is sama',[80] which means to hear, to listen and obey. The second, asa', means to do, to make, to be done or be made.[81] And the third, bad, to do, to make and to be carried out.[82]

Obedience is not, as we might think, a strict adherence to the letter of the Law. It does, of course, mean to obey, but more broadly to listen and to heed, to do what God asks of us, to carry out His orders. Obedience is asked for in the relationship to God, in the daily dynamic of a

---

[80] Goodrick&Kohlenberger III, *Zondervan NIV Exhaustive Concordance, 2nd Edition*, Zondervan Publishing House, Grand Rapids, Michigan, 1999, p. 1502, Strong's #9048

[81] Ibid, p. 1470, Strong's #6913

[82] Ibid, p. 1517, Strong's #10522. "bad" is an Aramaic word

partnership with God: Listening to God through Scripture and through the Indwelling Spirit of God. As I wrote in the Part I, we grow in love and trust of God if we will follow more faithfully His laws and especially the first four Commandments.

In fact, if we're in the right relationship to God, we cannot, and will not do anything that would displease Him or violate our own created nature. We would naturally follow all the laws about parents and neighbors. To listen and to obey God in all things is the goal. For now, in the first part of the wilderness, it is enough to be letter of the law people. Later we will learn to get beyond the rebellion and our fear of God's punishment, learning how to do everything out of love for God, out of the depth of our relationship with Him. Obedience is the first lesson of the wilderness.

The second lesson to be learned in the wilderness up to Mount Sinai is an absolute trust in the Lord to provide our needs, to lead us into the Promised Land and to love us. Our trust is not easily gained, because we are still on the lookout for a way out of this wilderness, a shortcut back to the world, another "god" to rescue us from God.

It is important to know that in the midst of the wilderness we can still hear God speaking to us; in fact, given our situation, we can hear God more clearly than we can when things seem to be going fine. On reader, K____, writes that: "About a year ago...I was dealing with an extremely rough situation...I started daily with fervent prayer and devotionals...one morning while sleeping I heard, 'Don't worry I'll lead you through the darkness.' The voice was very clear and distinct; it sounded like someone standing beside me, and woke me up. I wasn't scared but very aware of what was said. I do know this was a result of praying and asking for God's guidance."

Another reader, M____, was waiting for two weeks for a diagnosis after the doctors found a mass on her left lung. Fearful of cancer, the days were traumatic. One day while reaching inside the refrigerator for ice, she heard God say this: "DON'T WORRY, MY CHILD, I'VE GOT THIS!!!!" And the next day, stepping into the shower she heard the same voice saying "That I'm not leaving this world yet because He had things for me to speak about and that I was to share the miracles that He has given me...My sickness wasn't cancer and it was curable."

And there is God again at the end of Part II present to the Israelites, visible when Moses went into the Tent of Meeting. This is the first instance of His people worshipping in the wilderness after escaping from Pharoah's army at the crossing of the Red Sea; now they worshipped God while Moses talked to Him.

Moses stands for our soul –where God meets us-- while the people stand for all our rebellious parts, our ego. We worship while our souls commune with God.

Patricia Said Adams

Part III: From Egypt to Freedom

Chapter One:

Introduction, The Law

Part III covers Exodus Chapter 35 through Leviticus, Numbers and Deuteronomy

Introduction

The template that God left us in the Exodus story becomes really helpful in this second part of the wilderness where we are to bring our whole selves before God in love and service, to leave behind any self-centeredness or world-centeredness, any rebellion, and become totally God-centered. The rebellion of the Israelites and the laws which detail the Ten Commandments are the two major themes of the second part of the wilderness journey.

To move from rebellion to obedience takes a complete purging of ourselves and our worldly selves, so that we can enter the phase of *Illumination*, which comes towards the end of the wilderness story when we have let go of all rebellion. Illumination, "the experience of total consecration to God in love...[in which] God is given total control of the relationship,"[83] is the true preparation for entry into the Kingdom, into union with God. There is still an awareness of ourselves in the world, still slightly separated from God in the *Illumination* stage, which the Israelites achieved as they approached the River Jordan.

We let go of all the conscious areas of conflict with God in Part II. So what do we still need to purge? Now in Part III we're delving deeper into ourselves, beneath the surface to the subconscious and unconscious layers in order to bring our whole selves into conformity with God's ways and His laws. In essence we are giving up our attachments to the world's ways in order to live from our souls, where God dwells within us.

We will need to take responsibility for all of our unconscious attitudes, assumptions, and preferences many of which lie beneath the surface of our conscious minds. We need to make sure that we are totally aligned with God's will for us, with His laws, with our purpose, with God's love which intends to flow into us and back out again into the world, basically in gratitude for all that we've been given.

This second phase of purging is the hard work of the purgation process because we have to own all that we are,

---

[83] M. Robert Hulholland jr, *Invitation to a Journey: A Road Map for Spiritual Formation*, IVP Books, Downers Grove IL, 1993, p.94

all that has been done to us or happened to us, all that we have said and done. We are to purge ourselves, with God's help, of any tendency "to do wrong, miss the way," the meaning of the Hebrew word "hata" which is translated sin.[84] No longer can we just believe the tenets of our religion, we have to live them, too. We have to forgive ourselves and others. No more holding onto anything from the past, we are letting go of our pain and suffering, grief and shame, so that we can come into the present, into the presence of God.

No longer can we be "letter of the law" people, looking good on the outside, but sinful on the inside in our attitudes and judgments. We must embody the spirit of the Law as well. No longer can we ignore our own willfulness and rebellion. We have to accept and embrace all that we are, so that we can bring our whole selves to God in love; this was the core of Jesus' teaching in the first of His Two Great Commandments, ". . . to love the Lord your God with all of your heart, all of your soul, all of your mind and all of your strength."[85] Our adherence to the second of His commandments—to love our neighbor as ourselves-- is the proof that we are in alignment with the first.

It's not God who flinches at all that we are, but we ourselves who would hide the roots of our guilt and shame. God knows everything about us—how we think, what we've done, where we fall short, where we shine—so who are we hiding this knowledge about ourselves from? Ourselves and others! It is our job in this part of the wilderness to stand

---

[84] Goodrick & Kohlenberger III, *Zondervan NIV Exhaustive Concordance, 2nd Edition,* Zondervan Publishing House, Grand Rapids, MI, 1999, Strong's #2627, p. 1403
[85] Matthew 22:37. Luke 10:27 and Mark 12:30 differ from Matthew 22:37 by the addition of "with all your strength."

before God, naked of all attempts to hide anything about ourselves.

We have a great guide in this process: the Lord, Jesus, Christ, Holy Spirit, God—however you experience and name the Divine--who will highlight for us all the ways we fall short. Our task will be to own each thing and to lift it up to God for healing and transformation. If we are faithful to that task, our rebellious nature will slowly fade away and we will then be ready to cross the River Jordan into the Kingdom of God. It means not just letting God heal and transform us, we must apply our experience of His love and forgiveness for us to our own self-image; at long last we are accepting and embracing all that we are. And then, we can actually feel God's love and forgiveness for us. And when we can feel God's love for us deep in our bones, God's love for us flows back out to others, so that we are loving other people, too.

Our task in the later wilderness, therefore, is to offer up our whole selves to God. And it will be God's job to teach us His laws in detail, to transform our hidden selves so that we can bring our whole selves before Him. God will guide us in confronting the rebellious parts of us, allowing them to "die off," to be incorporated into our true self, the soul. Nothing that we are is lost, only transformed. And as that continues to happen, as we see how limited our own ways and our ability to see reality are, we will more and more allow God to direct our actions, our thoughts and our voice.

All the laws and all the experiences of the wilderness in Part III support this journey of the individual towards union with God. Chapter one includes this Introduction and the Law, a major focus of the 2nd part of the wilderness journey. The Law detailed in Exodus, Leviticus, Numbers and Deuteronomy is the breadth of the application of the Ten Commandments to God, ourselves and others. The theme of Chapter two is Rebellion and Obedience, how our rebellious human nature/our ego must be incorporated into the soul, so that God can lead us. Chapter three covers Purgation; it reveals the purification process by which we come into holiness which moves us from the supremacy of the world's influence, so that we are ready to enter the Kingdom of God.

Chapter four looks at our purpose. Chapter five examines what God is doing during these forty years in the wilderness and the stage of *illumination* at the end of those years. It looks at how God experiences our human nature and His response to it. Chapter six concludes the wilderness experience, which will focus on what we need to do during this longer time in the wilderness and how it benefits us and God. All the purgation, all the owning of who we are, all the giving up of our rebellion means that God can finally be in charge of our lives, in partnership with us.

The Law

God started handing down Commandments and laws about everything in the lives of the Israelites in Exodus before Moses went up to Mount Sinai to commune with God the first time[86] and continued throughout the rest of Exodus, Leviticus, Numbers and Deuteronomy. The laws handed are the major focus of these books. They expand on the Ten Commandments, the principles of the law, in great detail.

---

[86] Exodus 20: 1-ff

The laws cover worship, offerings, priests, servants and slaves, personal injury, property, social responsibility, justice and mercy, idols, the Sabbath, Festivals, the Tabernacle, diet, purification, the Day of Atonement, sin and holiness, the tribal camps and much more. They also define how life should go in the Promised Land.

In Deuteronomy 27 and 28[87] Moses outlines the blessings that accrue when we follow the Lord's commands and the curses that come if we don't. I think that the blessings and curses are not something that God sends us as we do something. He is not the vengeful God sitting in the chariot in the clouds just waiting with His thunderbolt to zap us. Be careful that you are not projecting your guilt and shame on to God and making Him a vengeful being. I believe that He built these effects and ramifications into the whole system of human behavior, so that if we choose to do what is right, then we are rewarded by that choice. We are freed from having to hide our actions, so we don't get caught. Also, we are able to see the good effect of what we do in ourselves and in others. We will see many blessings in everything we do. We can relax—there are no bad consequences.

If we do wrong, and continue to do wrong, we are piling up a whole litany of consequences just from making those decisions--paranoia, fear, self-protection, distrust and much more. We will be forever waiting for our punishment to fall on us, but, at the same time, working and hoping to avoid it.

---

[87] Curses: Deuteronomy 27:15-26, 28:15-68 Blessings: Deuteronomy 28:1-14

Both the blessings and the curses are the natural consequences of our choices. We could, if we wanted to, postulate with each decision we make whether it follows God's law or not. We could know with certainty whether we will be reaping positive or negative consequences. Obeying His laws, being true to Him, becomes paramount, if we want to enjoy our lives. What is being asked of us is not strict adherence to the letter of the law. What God is seeking is His law written on our hearts[88] so that we can follow the spirit of the law as well as the letter—that we would deal with ourselves and our neighbors in a spirit of love and mercy.

So many of the ancient laws of these four books of the Old Testament are directed at an agrarian society and seemingly have little to do with our urban, technologically savvy 21st century lives. Or they deal with areas of our lives like dietary prohibitions, which we no longer follow. Certainly, some of the laws apply to us. For example, in amplifying the commandment about giving false testimony against you neighbor, the writer of Exodus says, "Do not spread false reports" or be a "malicious witness." He goes on, "Do not follow the crowd in doing wrong...Do not deny justice to your poor people...do not accept a bribe."[89] In Deuteronomy it says that the judges "shall judge the people fairly."[90] And in Leviticus "do not pervert justice; do not show partiality to the poor or favoritism to the great, but judge your neighbor fairly. Do not go about spreading slander among your people."[91]

---

[88]Deuteronomy 30:14
[89]Exodus 23:1-8
[90] Deuteronomy 16:18
[91] Leviticus 19:15-16

Here is another group of laws that would apply to us today. The first is this: "Do not mistreat or oppress a foreigner, for you were foreigners in Egypt."[92] And again, "Do not oppress a foreigner, you yourselves know how it feels to be foreigners."[93] And later in Leviticus, "Do not mistreat them [foreigners]...Love them as yourself."[94] These reflect back to the Ten Commandments as well as Jesus' prescription "to love our neighbors as ourselves."[95]

Throughout our wilderness sojourn, God will be showing us the laws He wants us to follow. He'll be highlighting when we fall short. He'll be transforming our anger and fear into love, so that we can follow His laws.

Even if a lot of the laws don't seem to apply to us today, the principles of the law always apply whether it is the Ten Commandments themselves or the Two Great Commandments of Jesus.

God, through Moses, details these laws covering every aspect of the Israelites' lives, asking them (and us), ". . . to be holy to me because I, the Lord, am holy, and I have set you apart from the nations to be my own."[96] What does it mean to be holy? Qadas is the Hebrew word for holiness. It means to be sacred, consecrated, to be dedicated to, to be set apart for God. "By extension [sic.. it means to be] pure, innocent, free from impurity."[97] To be holy is to be wholly

---

[92] Exodus 22:21
[93] Exodus 23:9
[94] Leviticus 19:33-4
[95] Luke 10:27
[96] Leviticus 20:26
[97] Goodrick & Kohlenberger III, *Zondervan NIV Exhaustive Concordance*, 2nd *Edition*, Zondervan Publishing House, Grand Rapids MI, 1999, Strong's #7727 p.1482

set aside for God, to love Him with all of ourselves, to be so committed to Him that we could not violate His laws. Holiness means that we are totally God-centered. It is not just that we claim to be holy, but, in truth, there is nothing else but God that matters to us. There will be more about holiness in Part III, Chapter three.

I don't think that we have to go back to worshipping God in the ways of the Israelites or back to that much simpler life of three thousand years ago. But these four books of the Bible suggest that God is very interested in every detail of our lives, that He wants to be a part of, a partner to us, in everything. What are we to do today? It is in the daily, minute-by-minute listening to God that we hear what we need to know. Our dedication is not in any way to be limited to when we're in church on a Sunday: we are to partner with God in our families and other relationships, in our work, in our leisure and, yes, in the good works we do.

Here's where Jesus' Two Great Commandments summarize the spirit of the law. That everything we do should affirm our love of God with our whole selves and should show that love to the world through how we treat every person on this planet, each one of our neighbors and ourselves.

In order to love God with our whole selves, we must accept and embrace all that we are, all that we have done, all that was done to us. We must be free of attachment to our past. We must have forgiven all that we are, all that was done to us. Accepting and forgiving the past is a big step towards breaking the ties to the past. We must be able to live in the present moment where God is present, too. And we must accept our lives as they are, as a gift from God and live in gratitude for the great opportunity to live on Earth.

None of this are we capable of on our own. We need to lift every instance where we fall short of that wholeness, that partnership with God, to God that He might heal us and transform all that is the past, all that is not of God, in us.

Besides following the spirit of the law, we need to be open to a deep relationship with God, a partnership which embraces all that we are and all that we do. Righteousness, the Hebrew word "sedaqa" in the Old Testament means doing what is right in God's eyes, being in the right.[98] In the New Testament the Greek word is dikaiosyne,[99] which means being in the right plus having the right relationship with God.

It is in building this relationship through actively listening for the "still, small voice"[100] of the Indwelling Spirit of God in each of us, that we will receive all the instruction we will ever need for what we are to do and say, how we need to be, what still needs to be healed, what our next step is. It is a partnership for us with the One who knows us ever so much better than we know ourselves. It has been my experience in over thirty years of listening and heeding God's voice, that every single thing He has suggested is self-affirming, that is, affirming of my soul, not of my ego, thereby bringing it forward in my life, bringing me even closer to God.

---

[98] Goodrick & Kohlenberger III, *Zondervan NIV Exhaustive Concordance, 2nd Edition*, Zondervan Publishing House, Grand Rapids MI, 1999, p. 1478, Strong's #7407
[99] Ibid, p. 1542, Strong's #1466
[100] 1 Kings 19:12 KJV

To believe in God is only the first step on this journey. The task of the wilderness is to live what we believe, to have it inform every single thing that we do, to allow that belief to transform us, heal us, direct and sustain us. As we invest more and more of ourselves in that relationship and the deeper we go with God into ourselves, then our purpose is revealed. We'll talk more about purpose later in Part III, Chapter three.

In my own experience God has taught me so much from which way to drive home that day, to which restaurant to eat at for lunch to courses to take—photography, acting, magazine writing, to what to do now, who to call, what to say, which project to tackle first, which book to read next, and on and on. God is looking for a partnership with us in which we depend on Him for everything and He shows us the way to our whole, holy-created selves.

It is our obedience to the Law of God, the Ten Commandments, Jesus' Two Great Commandments, our willingness to do what God proposes to us, and our faithfulness to both that determines how far down this road to a deep relationship with God we will go.

As we begin to take in the love and forgiveness that God has for us—and we can do that as God heals our pain and suffering because we are now able to embrace who we are and know that we are lovable in God's eyes—God's love and blessings are pouring out to us and we, in turn, pour that same love and blessings onto our neighbors. This is the basic interchange in the world as God meant it to be. The more of us who are able to bring their whole selves before God, the more the Kingdom will be visible to our world's residents through the love we share everywhere we go.

Part III: From Egypt to Freedom

Chapter Two

Israelites and Rebellion

Rebellions — wanting to go back to Egypt, to live in the past

Even without the blessings and curses to tell if we're doing right or not, we have a huge problem in accepting God's love. No matter how many times the Bible talks about love and forgiveness, it's as if it doesn't apply to me. I can "know" that God loves me and yet, not allow Him to love me. Because of whatever guilt and shame I feel, I can hold God at arms' length, thinking that believing He loves me is enough. For how could God love as flawed an individual as I am? In reality, for all our profession of faith, and for all that God knows us better than we know ourselves, we still stand apart from God, holding Him at arm's length. The Israelites, the "stiff-necked"[101] people as God called them, these inconstant humans, are a good metaphor for our own rebellious nature.

There is something in us that says we have to be perfect before we come close to God. And clearly none of us is perfect enough to do that, so we continue to stand apart from Him. This is, of course, an illusion, because we live in God, God lives in us as the Indwelling Spirit of God, even if we are not aware of His presence. It takes a good part of the spiritual journey to put aside these false beliefs.

It is clear in reading the Exodus story that we are very much like the Israelites. We were all created in His image with free will, so we turn out to be inconstant, only not able to be faithful all the time. And this affects our self-concept, because we see God as a parent, the righteous One, even a vengeful One and we see ourselves failing to measure up to His standards.

So, given our own self-concept, we have to take Jesus' Great Commandments[102] as the standard. We are to bring our whole selves to God. That means that we have to accept all that we are, embrace who we are right now to do that. We have to forgive ourselves for whatever we've said and done. We have to acknowledge all that has happened to us in our lives. We have to forgive others for what they have done to us. We have to give up our rebellion. We have to own all that we are and have been.

[101] Exodus 32:9
[102] Luke 10:25-28

Then we can bring our whole selves to God in love. It may be that we can only embrace ourselves given the knowledge that God loves us, which we then apply to ourselves. And the proof positive of our love of God will be that we treat/love our neighbors as we treat/love ourselves. Only when we can acknowledge and accept all that we are can we come before God. And then we can acknowledge and love our neighbors, because they are the same flawed people that we are. To enter into a deep relationship with God means that we are no longer limited or intimidated by how we feel about ourselves, no longer trying to hide from ourselves, others and God.

Now we are living in truth, with integrity. We are transparent, hiding nothing. The inside of us—what was hidden before—is the same as what we present to the world. Here is the beginning of real humility. I am who I am. What you see is what you get. There is no inflation, nothing other than acceptance that I am like billions of other people, no better, no worse. And as I spend time with God and let Him direct my days, I realize that so much of the good in me comes straight from God. Straight from the place in me where God dwells in my soul. We've finally achieved the right kind of relationship with God. Here is where humility becomes our second nature. God loves me—all that I am, even me! How humbling is that? The Lord of the Universe can love me. And look at who I am, a flawed human being!

After the ultimate rebellion of building another god to take them back to Egypt detailed in Exodus 32, the Israelites still had not learned their lesson. Or, maybe it was just that generation which God led out of Egypt that could not remember all that God had done for them and so continued to rebel against Him. They were unable to give up their attachment to Egypt, so it colored everything that happened to them. And God meets each rebellion with some punishment.

In Numbers there are three instances of Israel's rebellious mood. In Chapter 11 the "people complained about their hardships in the hearing of the Lord, and when he heard them his anger was aroused. Then fire from the Lord burned among them and consumed some of the outskirts of the camp. When the people cried out to Moses, he prayed to the Lord and the fire died down."[103]

And that wasn't the end of it. "The rabble with them began to crave other food, and again the Israelites started wailing and said, 'If only we had meat to eat! We remember the fish we ate in Egypt at no cost—also the cucumbers, melons, leeks, onions and garlic. But now we have lost our appetite; we never see anything but this manna!'"[104]

While sometimes the rebellious Israelites were punished for their behavior, in this case the Lord first provided them with quail two cubits (3 feet) deep, then he struck the people ". . . with a severe plague."[105]

In Numbers 13, the Lord has Moses send out an advance party into Canaan to gauge the difficulties or ease of conquering that territory. Representatives of each tribe were sent. When ten of these twelve men reported back to the Israelites, they exaggerated the difficulties: "We went into the land to which you sent us, and it does flow with

---

[103] Numbers 11:1-2
[104] Numbers 11:4-6
[105] Numbers 11:33

milk and honey! Here is its fruit. But the people who live there are powerful, and the cities are fortified and very large." They continued with a report of all the peoples they had seen: descendants of Anak, Amalekites, Hittites, Jebusites, Amorites, and Canaanites. A suggestion was made to take possession of the land, but the men who had gone up with him said, 'We can't attack those people; they are stronger than we are.' And they spread among the Israelites a bad report about the land they had explored. They said, 'The land we explored devours those living in it. All the people we saw there are of great size…We seemed like grasshoppers in our own eyes and we looked the same to them.'"[106]

The people mourned their fate and grumbled against Moses and Aaron. Again, they cried out: "If only we had died in Egypt! Or in this wilderness! Why is the Lord bringing us to this land only to let us fall by the sword? Our wives and children will be taken as plunder. Wouldn't it be better for us to go back to Egypt?' And they said to each other, 'We should choose a leader and go back to Egypt.'"[107]

Joshua and Caleb who had been with the advance team said in rebuttal: "The land we passed through and explored is exceedingly good. If the Lord is pleased with us, he will lead us into that land, a land flowing with milk and honey, and give it to us. Only do not rebel against the Lord. And do not be afraid of the people of the land, because we

---

[106] Numbers 13:26-33
[107] Numbers 14:1-4

will devour them. Their protection is gone, but the Lord is with us. Do not be afraid of them."[108]

As the Lord is once again ready to kill off the Israelites because of their complaints, Moses reminds Him about His reputation among all the peoples. And so the Lord relents, but declares that not one of those whom He had rescued from Egypt will ever go to the Promised Land.[109] That whole generation will have to die off before the Israelites can enter Canaan. The members of the advance team were all killed except Joshua and Caleb who had told the truth.

Worse yet, the Israelites decided to conquer Canaan by their own will. The Amalekites and the Canaanites " who lived in that hill country came down and attacked them and beat them down all the way to Hormah."[110]

This incidence of rebellion was particularly damaging because the Israelites were not listening to God, but to their own will, so there was no way they could succeed. This part of the story I really resonate with, because when I started to write this book after doing all the research I thought was necessary in the fall of 2015, I found that I could barely write anything. After three days of trying, I heard this: "Don't! Don't do anything until you are inspired!" And so I set aside my will, my way of approaching this book. And I waited six months for that inspiration. In the meantime, I had signed

---

[108] Numbers 14 7-9
[109] Numbers 14:20-22
[110] Numbers 14:45

up for the School of the Spirit[111] which had a long, required reading list and a long supplementary one.

Since I had so much time on my hands without the book to write, I read most of both lists. And I found so many quotes that I could use in this book. I also began to understand that God was telling me that I was not ready to write this book, that something more had to happen in me, before I could write it. And so I waited, knowing that He was right. I trusted Him. Then, in the fall of 2016, I felt the go-ahead to write the book. So I wrote the second draft. And then, there was another period of time, three or four months long, when I awaited the inspiration to finish the book. I was clearly meant to write this book in God's timing and in His ways, not in mine!

Again in Numbers 20:1 at the Desert of Zin at Kadesh where Miriam died and was buried, the people again complained to Moses—"Why have you brought us out of Egypt to die in the wilderness?"

Then after Aaron's death, the people again complained to Moses. The Lord sent venomous snakes among them which bit them and they died. The people admitted their sin against the Lord and prayed that the Lord would take the snakes away. So the Lord told Moses, "Make a snake and put it up on a pole; anyone who is bitten can look at it and live."[112]

Later when they were in Shittim, some Israelite men succumbed to the invitation of Moabite women to indulge in

---

[111] thelydiagroup.com/school-of-the-spirit/
[112] Numbers 21:6-9

sexual immorality and to eat some of the sacrificial food for their gods. Twenty-four thousand Israelites died before Phinehas killed an Israelite man and a Midianite woman and the Lord withdrew the plague.

Obedience to God is essential, if we are to leave our attachments to the world and to follow God. As I said above, it is not our strict adherence to every dot and tittle of the law, that is, being a letter-of-the-law kind of people, but our willingness to follow God and to love Him so much that we would not do anything to disappoint or to detract from all that He is—this is the essence of the spiritual life.

Individual Disobedience

There are a number of stories in Leviticus and Numbers about direct disobedience to God by a few individuals. The general complaints by large numbers of Israelites about not being in Egypt were one thing; these instances were generated by individual choices.

In Leviticus 10 Aaron's sons Nadab and Abihu put fire in their censers, added incense and "offered unauthorized fire before the Lord, contrary to his command. So the fire came out from the presence of the Lord and consumed them, and they died before the Lord."[113] To explain His reaction to Moses, God said this: "Among those who approach me/ I will be proved holy;/ in the sight of the all the people/ I will be honored."[114] The laws He had handed down were to be followed, thereby honoring Him.

---

[113] Leviticus 10:1-2
[114] Leviticus 10:3

Later in Leviticus, the son of an Israelite mother and Egyptian father cursed the name of the Lord. He was stoned to death.[115]

And then in Numbers when Miriam and Aaron opposed Moses because he had married a Cushite wife. "Has the Lord spoken only through Moses?" they asked. "Hasn't he also spoken through us?"[116] The Lord was furious because Moses ". . . is faithful in all my house!"[117] When the Lord left them, "Miriam's skin was leprous…white as snow."[118] Aaron asked Moses to intercede with the Lord about their sin. The Lord left the leprous condition for a week on Miriam.

When a man was found gathering wood on the Sabbath, he was stoned to death. [119] When Korah, Dathan and Abiram became insolent towards Moses and rebelled with 250 Israelite men, the ground under those three split apart and swallowed them up along with their households and all those associated with Korah and their possession. Fire consumed the 250 men. Then a plague was sent.[120]

Moses' one act of rebellion in forty years of being God's spokesman to the Israelites, sealed his fate. He was not to be allowed into the Promised Land. He would die just short of the Jordan River. And what had he done? Early in the wilderness the Lord had asked him to speak to the rock at Kadesh, so that it would pour out its water for them. With

---

[115] Leviticus 24:10-23
[116] Numbers 12:1-2
[117] Numbers 12:7
[118] Numbers 12:10
[119] Numbers 15:32-36
[120] Numbers 16

the Israelites about him grumbling again about the lack of water, Moses struck the rock instead. The water spewed out, but Moses lost any chance of entering Canaan.[121]

When we turn to Part IV, we'll see one more act of rebellion just after the Israelites conquered Jericho. That will be in Part IV, Chapter One: The Israelites.

It is clear that the Lord is punishing any rebellion against His laws. Later in Deuteronomy[122], He makes it clear that to follow His commands brings blessings and to disobey brings curses. The punishment is usually swift and fatal. The adherence to what God asks of us, unlike the lies of the advance team's report on Canaan, brings blessings and successful campaigns against the kings in Canaan.

And what, you may ask, do the rebellions of the Israelites have to do with our journey with God? Well, the Israelites represent humanity in this story: We are as stiff-necked and rebellious as they were, as inconstant as they were in our ability to keep our attention on God. And this is what we must face about ourselves: that, in spite of what we profess to believe about God, we are more apt to complain about this event or that suffering, to be impatient with God in not answering our prayers, to continue to rely on our own resources rather than on God. We are apt to be ungrateful for our lives, to reject any suffering or inconvenience. So rather than embracing our lives as they are, here in the wilderness, we are apt to complain and wish for another kind of experience, definitely easier and more to our taste.

[121] Numbers 20:1-12
[122] Deuteronomy 28

And we depend more on ourselves and our way of accomplishing things than on God.

Our rebelliousness has to go. *God cannot use us as long as we hang on to our free will.* With free will we get to pick and choose what we want to do and what we don't. *God is asking us to just accept what comes to us and deal with it in partnership with Him, to align our free will with His will.* With free will we can ask God for what we want. *God is asking us for all of ourselves.* With free will we can still go our own way whenever we choose. *God is asking us to do things His way: with love, in the right timing.* With free will we can stay attached to the past, nurse our grievances, not forgive ourselves or others, or even God. *God is asking us to come into the present with Him, to forgive ourselves and others as He has forgiven us, to forgive Him for what we think He should have done.* With free will we can control how much God will ask of us by only giving Him part of ourselves. *He wants us wholly, deeply committed to Him.*

I turned off the radio in my car over a year ago and have become really acquainted with how I think and how I respond to situations, like the cars ahead of me. Are they going to cause any harm to me, how much anger there is in my thinking and much more. It's been a revelation to me to just be with my thoughts. I have become an observer of them, but I work at not getting embroiled in the emotions they try to evoke. So I am serene while they would have me raging. I dream up so many scenarios and what I would shout at the drivers who caused me to slow down, or who made me wait for them to turn or who cut in front of me. I had no idea that my thoughts would prod me to react badly to so many things.

As I get acquainted with how I think, particularly when I am on high alert as I drive, I can see the thoughts for what they are. I now see that I have a filter, which looks for any threat to me, any time I think circumstances won't work out for me. And that filter is assuming facts not in evidence, but judging them nonetheless. After seeing how I anticipate events, which never come to pass for a few months, all I can do is laugh at the paranoid thoughts I am casting on the future.

If all of us are projecting disaster for ourselves on what might happen—these are issues that define what attachments we have to the culture, to the world, to our own selves most of all, as opposed to being in God's Kingdom. As I write these words I keep seeing Adam and Eve just walking in the garden with God, communing with Him, enjoying the fruit of His Kingdom. With our free will and our rebellious nature we have to choose to go back into the garden, to align our free will with God's will once again. Eden bookends our lives if we will let it. First, we've been tossed out of the garden for not obeying God. And now He is inviting us right back into that same garden, now referred to as the Kingdom, if only we will step back into that obedience to Him, listening to Him, heeding what He asks of us.

As we work with the Lord, as He teaches us in this second part of the wilderness what is required of us, we need to be asking that He heal our rebelliousness, that He help us take our free will and freely apply it to following God's will for us in all things. He promises us a full life, a rich relationship with Him, freedom and peace and joy and love and all the fruit of the Spirit[123] if we will undertake with God the healing of the unconscious assumptions, expectations and presumptions in our thinking and just plain let them go. What we will be left with is an openness to what God is doing in our lives, an availability to God in all that He desires of us. In return, we relax our hyper-vigilance about our own safety and survival in favor of totally trusting in God's providence and care for us. And finally, we will be free of all the conditioning that does not belong to us!

From Rebellion to Obedience

During this longer time in the wilderness, we see the Israelites begin to take the necessary steps away from rebellion into obedience to God. Shortly after the debacle with Baal, God through Moses begins to lay down all sorts of details about creating the Ark, the Tabernacle, the Table, the Lampstand, altars and more.

"Then the whole Israelite community withdrew from Moses' presence, and everyone who was *willing and whose heart moved them* came and brought an offering to the Lord for the work on the tent of meeting, for all its service, and for the sacred garments. "All who were *willing*, men and women alike, came and brought gold jewelry of all kinds: brooches, earrings, rings and ornaments. They all presented their gold as a wave offering to the Lord."[124] [Italics added.] They brought yarn or linen, goat hair, ram skins, silver and bronze and acacia wood. Those who had the right skills helped: women spun goat hair and linen. They brought gems for the ephod and breastplate. Spices and olive oil for anointings

---

[123] John 10:10, Galatians 5:22-3
[124] Exodus 35:22

and for incense. And freewill offerings for the work. And more.[125]

So the first step into obedience is taken: a willingness to follow and to obey God. To be willing means to have one's heart moved.

The second step is to hear from God about our purpose. In the context of the Exodus story the purpose for many was to build the sacred elements and to take care of them. Our talent and abilities set our purpose in many instances, but there is also the experience we have gained from our pain and suffering and how we can offer that to the greater community.

The third step is to stop rebelling, to claim our own rebelliousness. This was a much longer process. First, God declared that these stiff-necked people, those who kept complaining, the ones He had rescued from slavery in Egypt, would not see the Promised Land, they would die before the younger generations crossed the Jordan. To grumble and complain, to hang on to the desire to return to Egypt as the place where all their needs were met, to try to conquer another tribe without God's help, to lie about Canaan and its peoples, to desire to worship other gods, to blaspheme, to oppose Moses, to be insolent, to indulge in sexual immorality, to exercise one's own will in worship, to work on the Sabbath—all these rebellions have to go. These are all ways of exercising our own will and ignoring God's will.

---

[125] Exodus 35:22-29

Finally, the rebellion stopped, as the older generation died off. It was in the episode with the snakes in Numbers 21 that the Israelites admitted they had sinned. And still they fell out of God's will with the Moabite women!

The fourth step into obedience is to see the effects of all we do on the greater community. The Covenant with the Israelites is with the whole tribe. And so it is with us: We are called to contribute to the Kingdom, to the whole body of Christ, to our individual congregations, to any group in our midst and to individuals. But the call is to serve the whole people of God, not just any one group, certainly not just those who are like us.

The story of Balak, king of Moab and Balaam, which takes up books 22-24 of Numbers, underscores the absolute necessity of taking the fifth step into obedience: to listen to what God is saying to you and to do exactly what He asks. Balaam was apparently a prophet and a non-Israelite who is asked by Balak to curse the Israelites, so that the Moabites can overcome them. But Balaam, in seven messages from the Lord, refused to curse the Israelites and in fact, he prophesized that God was with Israel and they would be successful against the Moabites, the Edomites, the Amalekites, the Kenites and Ashur and Eber.[126]

Obedience to the Law itself and to the Spirit of the Law is what is being asked of us. It's no good to be nice to people or to serve the homeless and to not pour out God's love to them. To observe the Spirit of the Law means that

---

[126]Numbers 22-24

our hearts, minds, souls and strengths are all aligned in serving God.[127]

---

[127] Matthew 23:23-24

Part III: From Egypt to Freedom

Chapter Three

Purging, Holiness, Purpose, Illumination

Purging into Holiness

Purging all of our "stuff"(giving up our rebellion) will lead us to *Illumination*, the third step of the spiritual journey after *Awakening* and *Purging*. Purgation is a "state of pain and effort," of detachment from the world of sense.[128] With illumination the soul is awakening to knowledge of reality. "Now it looks upon the sun."[129] Somehow in this illuminative state the soul retains its identity in the world.

---

[128] Evelyn Underhill, *Mysticism,* Dover Publications, Mineola, NY, 2002(1930 originally, 12th edition). P. 169
[129] Ibid

"It [illumination] is a sustained state in which it is easier to pray, give up things that are superfluous or obstruct progress, and work to accomplish more for the Kingdom of God...Perhaps the most discouraging part of the illuminative way is not the envy of others, but the revelation of our own inner turmoil."[130] And yet it is easier to give up all this struggle and ambivalence than to hang on to it. In the Illumination stage our prayer life changes from this: "A measuring of self against the teachings of the Gospel... now gives way to a gentle dialogue with Christ, characterized more by substance than by words." [131] This is more a resting in Christ or being in His mind than the lifting up of all the places we fall short that marks the purgation stage. It is not until the unitive state that our identity is lost in God's. We'll address that in Part IV.

The whole purpose of the purgation stage of the spiritual journey is to bring us to holiness, ". . . because I, the Lord your God, am holy."[132] Those who follow the Lord are to be consecrated, set apart, dedicated to God so that we could be "pure, innocent, [and] free from impurity." [133] Our holiness before God is a primary issue for the Lord who is holy. In many passages in the Exodus story, He called upon the Israelites to be holy, to be His sanctified people.[134]

---

[130] Benedict J. Groeschel, *Spiritual Passages: The Psychology of Spiritual Development,* The Crossword Publishing Co., New York, 1983, p. 138-9

[131] Ibid, p. 140

[132] Leviticus 19:2

[133] Goodrick & Kohlenberger III, *Zondervan NIV Exhaustive Concordance,* 2nd Edition, Zondervan Publishing House, Grand Rapids, Michigan, 1999, Strong's #7705, p. 1481

[134] For Example: Exodus 22:31, Leviticus 20:7, 26, Deuteronomy 7:6, 14:2, 21, 26:19, 28:9, 33:1-3

The first part of being holy is to cleanse oneself of all the "stuff," all the self-centeredness, which means that we can come before God purely ourselves as He created us to be. All the resistance to God, all the rebellion, all the me - first attitudes, all the cultural attitudes have been let go of. We stand naked before God, listening, heeding, praying, now unencumbered. Light. Free. Ready for whatever comes.

The second act of holiness is to come totally under the Law. To love God with all our heart, soul, mind and strength means that we could not, would not do anything that would offend our God in any way. This does not mean an exacting accounting of each law and how we followed it, but rather it is bringing all of ourselves under the law, not just our actions, but our attitudes. And that depends on purging ourselves of all that is "not of God."

Purging and purification are themes in the forty years in the wilderness. Laws cover what to do with defiling skin diseases, the aftermath of birth for the new mother, dietary restrictions: clean and unclean foods, ritual cleansings, circumcision and more. Coming before God, living the life in which we live in God's arms all the time requires a purity, a holiness, an attitude towards God of open abandonment to Him—everything else is purged from our state of being.

In addition to the rituals for cleansing and purification in the Exodus story, a whole chapter, Deuteronomy 28 is devoted to God promoting the idea that if we are obedient to God, blessings will accrue to us; if we aren't obedient, then we will be cursed. Built into our choices in life are the consequences thereof: In great detail Deuteronomy 28 lists the type of actions that will bless or curse us, depending on our obedience to God. The choice is ours—if we keep God's laws, we will be blessed; if we are not keeping God's laws, we will be cursed.

These choices are built into life here on Earth, as are the consequences. We ourselves choose to be blessed or cursed. God is not ready to zap us or to bless us with each choice that we make; He is not the huge Father sitting in His chariot in the sky ready to shoot off a thunderbolt in case we need to be cursed. He can sit back and watch how our lives unfold according to the way He designed the universe, in particular, how we choose to live—being blessed or being cursed. But, then, He is always there inviting us to live a God-centered life, wherein we will be blessed.

It is built into the system of human relationships and God that if we follow His laws we will be blessed.[135] It's really as simple as that. It's not as if God is just waiting for us to do wrong, so that he can zap us or to do right, so He can bless us; don't project that onto God. Especially, do not project our own punitive ways onto God. But He does set the standards by which we are to act. The closer we adhere to His law and to listening to Him, the more we will enjoy His blessings. That's the deal.

Alternately, if we refuse to follow this good counsel, then we will be cursed.[136] We will live in fear, paranoia even, always looking back over our shoulder to see if someone is after us. There will be confusion, illness, defeat and many other curses. These punishments are the direct result of our choices. Choose life, not darkness. Choose blessings,[137] not

---

[135] Leviticus 26:1-13, Deuteronomy 4:1-14, Deuteronomy 11:1-15, Deuteronomy 28:1-14
[136] Leviticus 26:14-39, Deuteronomy 27:9-26, 28:15-68
[137] Deuteronomy 28:1-14

curses.[138] It is totally up to us what befalls us. That is not to say that if we choose blessings, we will not be challenged or suffer. It is the nature of life here that we all experience pain and suffering. But we will still enjoy God's blessings through our difficulties, as well as God's presence seeing us through anything.

And He promises us that it is not so difficult to follow His Law: "Now what I am commanding you today is not too difficult for you or beyond your reach…No, the word is very near you; it is in your mouth and in your heart so you may obey it."[139] And then He sums up what He asks of us: "Now choose life, so that you and your children may live and that you may love the Lord your God, listen to his voice and hold fast to him. For the Lord is your life, and he will give you many years in the land that he swore to give to your fathers, Abraham, Isaac and Jacob."[140]

The second stage of the spiritual journey, *purgation*, ends in our conversion:

1) From our attachment or slavery to the world in favor of an attachment to God and His ways,

2) From our rebelliousness and complaints to an alignment with and obedience to the will of God,

---

[138] Deuteronomy 28: 15-68s
[139] Deuteronomy 30:11-14
[140] Deuteronomy 30:19-20

3)   From being completely separate from God to being completely captured by God and His vision for our lives.

Let me illustrate that conversion with some examples from my readers about their shift in perspective, their own sea change from a world's perspective to God's.

If we let God lead our lives, He will show us a new way of doing and being in the world. Here is a story of God's teaching A_____ a better way of relating to her husband soon after they both converted to Christianity. "I was driving my husband to work and I was arguing with him and as I was leaving where I dropped him off [at] work I got a speeding ticket. I knew right away that God was saying to me, 'Do not talk to your husband that way, treat him with love and respect.' So I received that ticket for speeding and I knew that it was God that sent that police officer to give me that speeding ticket, because I was not obeying our Lord. I was being my old self arguing and cutting him down, and it was like the Lord touched my heart and said, 'Love your husband and stop walking in the flesh.' "

Here is how B____ experienced that conversion: "Have you ever been really struggling with something, a task, routine, joy, relationship, addiction, financial problem, etc. and just felt worn out, exhausted and just plain overwhelmed. I have and never realized what a blessed state I was really in. Let me explain: See, all these issues used to really frustrate and sadden me, my focus was on the storm and it was overwhelming. But as I study Scripture and change my focus to the Master of the storm, a wonderful thing happens. The Holy Spirit starts to open my understanding of the Word and forgiving my spirit with His fruits. The waves of the storms start to calm and that 'still, small voice' [of 1 Kings 19:12] in my mind starts to thank and praise the Lord....now I'm welling up with joy like a river. I'm getting overwhelmed with God's goodness."

He has learned to focus, not on the storm, but on the Master of the storm who takes care of everything! He has learned to totally trust the Lord in everything.

C_____ experienced that conversion in a different way. Here is his story. "To me it was going broke a few times. I did fairly well in my profession, when something went wrong something [else] would open up and I would always be able to make more money. I really got arrogant. I thought it was me opening these doors. Then it all went south, no money to be made, credit rating went because of defaults. Then I started realizing who had been opening those doors for me. I slowly built back with God's help and guidance; now I am not so arrogant. I have decent credit, not like it was, but I don't need that. I get by, but it is in God's will, my dependence is on Him not myself." He had to face himself and put himself in God's hands when his work went south. This is a great example of moving from dependence on our own selves to dependence on God.

Our conversion and transformation does not happen just because we want it; it happens because we turned to God for help. We are not capable on our own of accomplishing the transformation in us. We don't know how to heal ourselves. We can't. Only when we are willing to listen to God and ask for His help, will we begin to change.

D_____chose to start changing her life fifteen years ago. "I wanted a closer relationship with God. My children were my inspiration. I'm now forty-six years old and life has taken me down some roads that I never imagined I would've gone. But God. I pray continuously on a daily basis. I'm going through my most challenging storm right now, but I can see the light ahead of me…I've beaten breast cancer, so anything else in life is a piece of candy."

Even giving up drugs and alcohol doesn't mean a complete conversion. Here is E____'s story: "God has set me free from drugs and alcohol; I was in that life style for 25 years of my life and even after coming to Christ in 1985, I still had that inner struggle with addiction and not liking myself that well. I had a clean time in my life and no foundation in Christ and then I married someone that was not God's will for me. Within a year we were getting high and not going to church or serving God like I promised Him." It would take some time before E___ got back on a good footing with God.

And God can ask some pretty difficult things of us. G____'s story went like this. When her father who drank a lot and her mother separated, she was being pulled in two directions, to side with one parent over the other. "I made up my mind to be more like my grandfather and focus on something far more personal than the feud and I chose Christ over the feud. Not long after giving my heart to God, He spoke audibly to me that to be His completely and receive His blessings in my life… I had to lay on the altar my cigarettes and lighter and give them up. So being obedient I did so, then before I left the altar again He spoke audibly to me and said, 'Now you must go home and confess your sin and sacrifice to your parents'...I battled it, but when I did so, my father refused to talk to me; he got up and went to his bedroom and I did not see or talk to him for three days and four nights. Come Sunday morning I heard him calling me. I went to see what he needed. He was dressed in his Sunday best and he said we are gonna be late to church if you don't get a move on...Shocked, I dressed and sure enough my parents went to the service with me and my father dedicated his life to Christ...plus my mother. He never drank again." Purging her addiction to cigarettes and confessing her sin and sacrifice to her father was a blessing for both her father and mother and for her.

For H____, whose father had died when she was 7 and who never felt loved, went into recovery [years later] and ten days later accepted Jesus Christ as her Lord and Savior. "Things didn't change immediately for there was way too much damage and character defects that needed much attention including my children. But first I need to get right with God. I did and He gave me the strength to overcome many obstacles which I put in my own way as well as learning the true meaning of love, I found peace and rest in my soul in God calling my father back home [when I was seven] and [I am now] free from my past, of all that haunted me. My heart, my mind, body and soul are set free to be and walk with God today."

"Things didn't change immediately" is a true statement for most of us. It takes time to turn the tide of a whole lifetime towards the Kingdom of God. It is not a quick or easy turnaround.

Even with someone whose life was given to Jesus at 27, the full, true conversion may come much later. For J____

141

the issue came when the doctors discovered a tumor on her husband's bladder. Finally, they said the bladder had to come out. Her husband got really depressed and all she could do was "cry and pray until I couldn't take it anymore. I told God [that] I lift him up to do whatever he needed to do. He already knew what was best and loved him more than I did. Finally, I felt like I did the right thing…gave him to God totally to do what he wished. He was in surgery for 11 hours. I trusted God totally. He got really sick. His stomach was so big I thought it was going to explode. On the 6th night he was in horrible pain and everyone was running around trying to figure out what was wrong.

'I bowed my head to pray. When I looked up Jesus was hovering over him. His eyes were looking down at his stomach with such power…Wonderful, wonderful power…He was wearing a white robe with a purple sash around his neck. I saw his feet, his hair and the power in His eyes. I blinked and he was gone. My husband continued to be very sick and hurting until the next morning early, when he asked me to help him sit up. I have no idea what made me grab a pan, but he threw up like I have never seen--black ugly stuff and he filled it. I ran for the nurse after I helped him back down. When I walked back into that room everything had changed. The pain was gone. From morphine to Tylenol in 5 minutes. I know what happened. My faith, love and trust in God has changed my whole life. I try to turn everything over to him now. It took me a long time to figure out why me. Why was I allowed to see Jesus. I'm no one, but feel so very blessed. I am His daughter and very happy about that."

When we are in a true crisis, we are often more open to God than when things are going well. In good circumstances we often think we need Him less, that we can be in charge.

Sometimes I think we are born into the wilderness. Here is a story of a child, K____, who was given all kinds of drugs from the age of four on by her drug-addicted mother and her friends. And she grew into an adult addicted to just about everything but IV drug use. Somehow, "through it all...I knew that I was never alone...[Finally when she got hooked on heroin she] was terrified...So I began fervently crying out to the Lord 2 years ago. During every drug deal I made, every line that went up my nose. I knew that there was nothing, as a lowly human, that I could do for myself. Well...let me just tell you that one year ago today, God reached down in the darkest, fiery pit of hell and snatched me out and called me forgiven and redeemed... I want you to know that we are all born from sin into sin, but we have One Creator and He loves each and every one of us so much that He will go into hell and save you, if you just believe and ask Him...Today I glorify God for my struggles knowing how much torment that I have endured giving into sin is nothing compared to the struggles that Jesus endured denying sin...I pray for God to use me mightily!!!"

What keeps us in the wilderness might be anger and a lack of forgiveness of old, old stuff. L_____ tells her story: "For 45 years I carried a burden of anger against someone who hurt me at a very young age! God allowed us to reconnect and for him to apologize to me! I forgave him! He forgave himself, I believe, because he said he had no regrets about his life but he was so sorry for hurting me! He opened up about so many things about his childhood that would explain why he behaved the way that he did! It was as if the flood gates opened up for him and I was there to listen! My life came full circle! I was free to move on! I loved him dearly for 45 years. Sadly, he died two days after that talk! I was in shock for two days! Then God stepped in and comforted me and gave me His peace! I was able to finally let go and close that book. I thank God for the time that He gave us to come to terms with everything and may he rest in peace!!"

Conversions happen in all different ways and for all different kinds of reasons. Sometimes, as it happened to M____, it was a new understanding that opened up how he thinks about God. For him, it was acknowledging that he had been considering God only in nature, in the physical world as Creator, but nothing else. "I found I wasn't acknowledging God's Word from a Spiritual perspective, but [only] from a Natural perspective, and after I found the Truth in John 4:24 ("God is spirit, and his worshipers must worship in the Spirit and in truth."), the Holy Spirit held me there until I perceived what was being revealed to me... to come to know the True Divine, unchanging, unadulterated and uncompromising true word of God." Such a change in the description of the God he worships!

The most dramatic conversions can happen with addicts, maybe years after they become addicted. N____ "had a beautiful spiritual awakening when I was at a sober living home. Jesus felt my shame and called my name. I've been clean and sober almost two years." For P___ "Once I got clean and sober my husband found a little grey 'military' book. After two weeks of him reading it...I realized it was a pocket Bible of the New Testament. It just blew me away! Learning of Jesus, His disciples, Paul and even Revelations, I could not believe how simple it was, to be saved! To accept Jesus as the Son of God, repent of our sins, and to spread the Gospel throughout the world! I never knew what reborn meant—I always thought it was some new agey thing, goodie two shoes...Wow! It all fell into place!! I understand! God created the Earth for Him and man to dwell. He will be our God and we will be His people. Love God with all your heart, mind, soul, strength."

T_____ was a young addict who had grown up Catholic. "Some things happened in my life and at a young age I lost myself in high school with drugs and alcohol; from ages 16-22 I was in a fog. Went to my first AA meeting at 22, bounced around for a while trying to work the steps and find out who God was/is in my life. My Mom died at 49 from cancer in June 1992; I got sober and surrendered in December 1992. Six months later my younger brother died...playing basketball caught an elbow and his carotid artery detached. He died two days later almost a year to the day of Mom ['s death]. Since them my faith has strengthened, sobriety is now 23 years!! Still every day I turn to God early and often. He is my Rock!!!

Or conversions can happen in a jail: O_____ "had an encounter with the Lord Jesus Christ within cement walls of the county jail here in _____ Florida and I have never been the same since...the Lord spoke to me about forgiveness, about forgiving myself, because He had already forgiven me."

Forgiving ourselves and others who have hurt us is a deeper way of purging the past than simple acceptance of what happened. Forgiveness clears out "our story" that has defined who we are. Being able to forgive ourselves or another person heals so much of our pain and suffering. After forgiveness there is a new spaciousness and freedom from the past, an ability to come into the present, into the presence of God.

Sometimes the church is the place for misunderstandings and for hurt. A new Christian woman, R_____, left the church she had been baptized in the spring before. She felt misunderstood and judged by other members without them seeking to understand her at all. "Through it all I have felt hurt, and abused in ways, and treated unfairly. I have become bitter and unforgiving and that is rebellion! I couldn't understand how to forgive people when they weren't sorry...I feel that God has been using every piece of this mess, allowing it into my life from His omniscience, omnipresence and omnipotence to bring me where I need to be as a Christian...The wilderness is just a part of the path that God brings us through...to remove what needs removing, and to build what needs building! For a month or two and maybe all along, God has told me to quit fighting! BE STILL AND KNOW THAT I AM LORD! I wanted to make them suffer...I don't get to tell Him what is right...I needed to learn that He will punish who He punishes, and He will have mercy on who He will have mercy! He is God, I am NOT! I don't like releasing control, but I never had it to begin with! My control was just an illusion to make me feel better, when in reality God being in control is the peace I've been seeking!"

S_____ drifted away from the church when he "allowed the bad actions of a few to shake my faith." Later he had moved to a new area and found himself "in one heck of a jam and couldn't figure a way out on my own. Not being the type to ask others for help, I broke down and asked family and a few new friends for help...but the Lord showed His presence SO abundantly that He himself placed me exactly where I needed to be to allow His grace to help simply by the Christian people He put me in contact with, first one person then another. We all felt God's presence to the point that four [virtual] strangers ALL began to tear up. The last week and a half of my life has changed my whole outlook about pretty much everything. But it especially has showed me without a doubt that no matter how far I have fallen from grace in the last few years, God never turned His back on me. I didn't realize until now how much I really miss God and need Him."

The second part of the wilderness is where these deeper, more painful areas of our lives are brought to the surface of our minds, so that the past pain and suffering can be healed, transformed by God. All we can do is to acknowledge where we are with these memories and offer them up to God to heal. Often our inability to deal with the past, where we can't forgive ourselves or another for what happened to us, brings us more pain and suffering than to the other person. It keeps us in the pain, reliving the story, unable to let it go. But here in the wilderness our stories stand starkly in our minds because God is asking us to let Him heal, to transform, to let go of all the pain and suffering that keeps us in the past and away from His influence and strength and love. As we are able to let these old stories go, as we let go of their influence on us, we come into a freedom, a grace that Jesus promised us when He said: "Come to me, all you who are weary and burdened, and I

147

will give you rest. Take my yoke upon you and learn from me, for I am gentle and humble in heart, and you will find rest for your souls. For my yoke is easy and my burden is light."[141]

One great side effect of the purging is the restoration of integrity in us. We are no longer saying one thing and doing the other. Or saying things that belie our emotions and thoughts. Our thoughts and our actions are aligned in harmony. We no longer have any reason to hide anything about ourselves. We just are who we are. Warts and all. Goodness and all.

It is a relief to come to the end of the wilderness, to approach the last physical barrier, the River Jordan, to our entry into the Promised Land. It's a relief to just rely on God, to trust Him in everything that we face, no longer to hold Him off at arm's length. We can catch a glimpse of our new "home" and can finally imagine what living in the Kingdom will be like. We finally can see the cost of all our rebellion, all the hidden parts of self, all the pain and suffering we would not share, all because we so depended on ourselves and not on God. We now trust God that when we follow His Word, He takes care of us. That when we face the enemies in Canaan, we will prevail. That the last crossing of the waters will bring us empowerment of the Holy Spirit. And oh, so much more!

---

[141] Matthew 11:28-30

Part III: From Egypt to Freedom

Chapter Four

Purpose

Purpose:

As we acknowledge all within us that rebels against God, all that stands apart from God, the next thing to be addressed for each of us is our purpose. Many of the laws that God handed down at Mount Sinai and beyond were about assigning jobs to whole tribes and to individuals as well, delineating each one's purpose. The intent of these laws was to award work to those who were gifted in certain trades, perhaps even to enhance these gifts, and also to organize the tribes so that they didn't have overlapping responsibilities; they could specialize in certain things. Clearly this happened with the Levite tribe, which was assigned to assist the priests.

First, there would be a census. And then each tribe would be assigned neighbors and where to camp. For instance, the tribe of Issachar, a division of Judah was to camp next to the camp of Judah on the East side of the camp. And then the tribe of Zebulun. To the south would be the camp of Ruben. And so on.[142] Then each tribe was appointed certain tasks; the tribe of Levi was to assist Aaron the priest.[143] One of the branches of the Levites, the Kohathites, were assigned care of the most holy things.[144] The Gershoites, another branch, were assigned the care of the curtains for the Tent of Meeting, the Tabernacle, the courtyard.[145] The Merarites, again a branch of the Levites, would "carry the frames of the tabernacle, its crossbars, posts and bases"[146] and more.

As they prepared to move into the Promised Land, the Levites would not inherit any land, but had forty-eight cities set aside for them in Canaan. Thirteen belonged to the priests. The rest were for the remaining Levites. In addition, each city set aside some land for the Levites so they could raise cattle and crops for themselves.[147] The offerings to God would go onto the priests' plates.

Isn't it amazing how detailed were God's plans for the Levites and how cognizant He was of each individual's and each tribe's gifts and talents? He has the same kind of detailed plans for each of us.

---

[142] Numbers 2:3-10
[143] Numbers 3:1-51
[144] Numbers 4:4
[145] Numbers 4:21-28
[146] Numbers 4:29-33
[147] Numbers 35:2

God created each of us with certain gifts and talents. In addition, during our lifetime here on Earth we have learned a lot from the pain and suffering we've been through. God wants to use all that we are and all that we know for a purpose that all of us share: To make the Kingdom of God visible on this Earth. As Paul wrote to the Corinthians[148] "Now you are the body of Christ, and each one of you is a part of it. And God has placed in the church first of all apostles, second prophets, third teachers, then miracles, then gifts of healing, of helping, of guidance and of different kinds of tongues."

How each of us is to accomplish our purpose depends on God's intention for us in the first place—our gifts and talents—and on our experience in life. These three attributes will determine that purpose. Sometimes our purpose is obvious from a young age. A child has a gift for compassion; another for art; another for science. No matter the gifts and talents or how well they are developed, our purpose was set in our creation. Now, as we come to God in a deep relationship, as we come to be healed and transformed by Him, He begins to reveal our purpose to us.

E_____ shows how early on our inclinations might lead us to our purpose. "Growing up, I always had the gift of 'gab'. . . My parents said I never met a stranger. It holds true today. God has blessed me with the ability to make friends or comfort those in need. I was at a Joyce Myer Women's Conference in 2013 when God spoke to me ever so plainly and clearly, 'I've called you to teach, minister and comfort women.' I was like, I can't. He said, 'You can. My grace is sufficient to get you through.' I was shocked, scared,

---

[148] 1 Corinthians 12:28

and unsure of myself. I had always felt inadequate, less than, not good enough. He said I was more than enough because I belonged to Him.

"So for the past two years I've been stepping out more leading Women's groups at church and speaking at other churches. He has been amazing. Now, He is moving me to another church. I've had a hard time with this. I've been at this church my whole life. But when He says go, I have to go. So, in January, I'm moving churches. So in God I trust. Him I follow."

I can affirm her experience from my own. God's suggestions for me over the years have always left me a little breathless—they are just beyond what I think I am capable of, but not beyond my abilities with His help!

N____ heard God's purpose for her in this way: "He told me to be a teacher of music. I teach guitar for free and collect instruments for students who cannot afford them on their own. I also learned we are not born with guardian angels; He gives them to us when we ask." She's using her innate musical talent to teach others, for free!

Our purpose may be about how we are with God, more than how we are with other people. A____ reveals how our purpose might consist of how we do things rather than what we do. "In 2003 the Lord spoke to me in a dream; He told me that He wanted me to begin to praise Him for that which He is about to do. My response was okay and I started to walk away; at that point He took a hold of me and said, 'I want you to begin to praise ME for what I am about to Do. You praise ME for the things that I have done; and you praise me for the things I am doing; but I want you to begin to praise Me for that which I am about to do, and you don't have a clue what that is. Since that time I began praising the Lord night and day for that which He is about to do; and He has richly blessed me and my family and everyone that I have shared this dream with that praises Him for that which He is about to do, too."

Another example of one's purpose in support of others is in K_____'s story: "The purpose that I feel that God has given to me is to make a difference in someone else's life, to be happy and to help them turn their life around by having faith and being positive at all times, through any situation you have." L_____ has found that "yielding to the Holy Spirit has caused me to become adaptable for whatever purpose He has that day. That said, my purpose changes like the seasons to meet people where they are. My key purpose is to be a conduit for the Full Love of God in, through and out in abundant flow." These two women support the people they meet through crises and help them get back on their feet. I am sure that they profoundly affect the lives of those they help.

Here is a more counseling-based approach to helping others. M____ was ordained as an Evangelist. For her "my Kingdom purpose is love, seeking encouraging talents and gifts, and teaching with a counsel-like approach...Seeing folks realize their talents and gifts is super exciting to me. Teaching God's Word, taught to me by Holy Spirit mainly, gave me a tremendous appetite to teach others...When I am doing this I am most joyful."

Another reader, N_____, has become more aware of her gifts from God. She has vision. "I've questioned God on this before. I thought this really isn't happening; I may just be over-thinking the situation. God usually shows me that I'm correct [in] what I thought or felt was going on behind the scenes. I'm still praying for guidance on this gift. I don't always know when to speak on it. Also I am working and trusting God to help me with the first gift. At times I know I can use too many words and completely lose the person that is supposed to receive the personal message... I need God just like I need the air that I breath." Her story illustrates an important quality to have when fulfilling our purpose: humility. Our purpose is given to us by God, just as are the talents and gifts and experience required to fulfill that purpose. They are not bestowed to pump us up, but purely for the benefit of God, the Kingdom and all humanity.

Our purpose, gifts and talents are to be enjoyed by us in partnership with God. So we have to be tuned sufficiently to God's "still, small voice" of 1 Kings 19:12 in order to execute our purpose. It is in the relationship with God that we stay on track with our purpose, that we remain humble, that we put God first in our lives. Here's how O_____ put it: I write and move when God speaks. He is definitely preparing me for greater [things]. For His purpose. I have to drop everything at that moment and write [the idea down] if I want to capture what He's telling me." As a writer myself, I write everything down that God is telling me. If I'm in the car when an idea occurs to me, I capture it on Voice Memos on my phone. When I sit down to write about that idea, I can be assured that the whole thing will be fleshed out as I write and edit it.

Someone's purpose is not necessarily a job, but it can be. Here is how B_____ found her purpose: My husband and I were attending our church service and our pastor asked us to close our eyes and listen for the Lord to speak. We were fairly new members to this church. As I listened I only heard one word. Let me be clear. I did not hear a voice, it was more of a thought, but it was only one word. The word was 'children.' I can't really explain what I felt at the time except a sense and desire for obedience like I've never felt before. " As she left church that day she signed up to help in the Sunday School department. "I can't explain this, but that just wasn't it. A few weeks went by and I noticed that I was literally being bombarded by messages regarding foster care. I saw it on billboards, the side of buses, park benches, etc.

"Well, my husband and I took the classes and were foster parents for 12 years and I have never had such a rewarding experience. We are grandparents to 7 grandchildren now and even have one named after me. My husband developed heart disease and we had to quit fostering. I thank God for this blessing in my life and have realized after looking back at my life I have been involved with children since I was young myself…. I love when He opens my eyes to His purpose!" B____'s story also illustrates that purpose can be an evolving one. Now that they are done with fostering children, it's time to listen for what is next.

The story that P____ tells highlights the fact that we're not always asked to give out of our strengths and talents, but out of our weaknesses. "The Lord told me to [comment] on this one. He showed me my purpose is to love people and point to Jesus [as] the One making it possible [1 John 4:7]. That sounded simple to me, but I spent a whole lifetime looking for and wondering what my purpose was—in jobs, in talent, in relationships, etc., although I am gifted and blessed in many areas of my life. God choose the two things that I'm not very good at to bring glory to His name and Kingdom: loving people and talking --LOL. But through His grace I find great joy and peace just telling people about Jesus and His love for us. Now I can live happy and fulfilled just knowing that all I need to do is love people and tell them about Jesus."

A purpose may not be revealed for a while or it may evolve over time. I know that when I first started spiritual direction training, I had no indication that writing would eventually supplant that great love of mine. That took a good ten plus years to become clear. Of course, what I do write is from a spiritual director's point of view, so that whole training and experience is not lost at all. And I do supervise a few director's-in-training, so I still have a hand in it indirectly.

R____ is still waiting to hear what her purpose is. Her son committed suicide at 17. "I surrendered to God right away. I had never felt such pain and brokenness, ever! I started asking God why over and over again and after He answered me. I thought I was crazy, but then I began asking Him what He wanted from me, because I was lost and didn't even know who I was anymore; the person I was had just died! He, of course, started answering me, He started with the words 'Be Still and know that I am God!' and after I figure out it was a verse, I KNEW that I KNEW that it was God speaking to me. I found that I was always wanting to be alone so that I could hear Him speak to me. He told me He knew me before He formed me in my mother's womb; He set me apart for a purpose, that I was His handiwork. He reminded me that He gave us the air to breathe and that it is

His breath that gives us life and my purpose He will reveal in time! It's been seven years since the day my son went home to heaven and my husband and I are now reborn Christians and in our third and final year of Discipleship school. We are excited to see where God is leading us as His disciples.

Here's another story where the purpose became clear over time. A____ reports that, "My purpose is clear to me, clearer that it has ever been. God began a process with me more than twenty years ago, revealing my purpose a bit at a time, telling me all I needed to know in each moment. The key for me was to listen carefully, not so much with my ears, but more with my heart. The more I offered God my heart and soul, the clearer God spoke to me. God's revelation took me from offering myself to ministry through ordination…a missionary to Uganda, a hospital chaplain, a parish minister and a trauma specialist working with victims of violence and abuse. Today I am retired from career ministry, but my purpose has not changed. God is asking me to be present and mindful, exercising my faith through prayer and contemplation. God is leading me into writing and art. The result is a daily inspirational blog and a second blog for my watercolor paintings. My past has made my present much clearer, and I am in a place of peace."

So often I think that we have to be healed and transformed, or maybe it is only to be awakened before God will reveal His purpose for us. I have experienced that in writing this book. There have definitely been periods, months of time, when I was not to write anything, especially anything that came from me or my own priorities. By the time I was given the go-ahead by the Holy Spirit, I had been through a lot of old stuff—called to my attention by the Lord, and lifted up to Him for healing. Just one example will suffice. I've been reading a number of biographies and autobiographies of missionaries and other Christians, particularly from the 19th and 20th centuries. I feel that their stories have greatly enhanced my own dedication to God. But one book that I borrowed from my daughter was about a love story that was so deep and tragic—the missionary's wife died at a very young age. I read 50 pages in that book and couldn't read anymore. All I could think of was of my late husband and our life together—he died 16 years ago. I was shocked at the emotions I felt, because I thought I had thoroughly grieved his loss. That book mirrored what I was not aware of at all which needed to be healed before I could finish Parts III and IV of this book.

Here's another story where the woman was given the call to a purpose, but it took another eight years before she understood it: "Ye I set you down in the midst of my people as a plumb line. As they love you, so shall they love Me." At the time she did not have a relationship with God and no one else she consulted understood it, either, although one person said that "plumb line" was in the book of Amos. This year she spent Thanksgiving week alone with God in worship and prayer with what He had long ago said to her. She heard that He had called her to be a prophetess! The next Sunday in church a speaker stepped forward who was not scheduled to speak and spoke of the Gift of Prophecy. "I was stunned. This was the answer to my prayer. The message was very thorough and afterwards, I went up to be prayed over that my gift come forth. I knew this was a step in the process. Later the speaker told me that he was not originally scheduled to speak, but asked to give this message after he felt an overwhelming urge from God!"

For S_____ her purpose is to be God's cheerleader. "My prayers have been 'May Your light shine through me that others may come to know You.' Through a series of years, God has called me to simply be His cheerleader. Growing up in a violent home with alcoholic parents, giving my life to Christ at 19, marrying a young youth pastor, falling from grace into the depths of my own disease of alcoholism for 16 years. God moved suddenly in my life, striking me sober as I still sat on a barstool, accepting me with open arms like the return of the prodigal son and commissioning me to reach out to others in their darkness to share His mercy, love, compassion and grace! I am so very blessed to share His message of love by living in His will for me daily."

Often our purpose comes out of the suffering we have experienced and have been healed of. A "wounded healer" might be an ex-addict who works with addicts, an ex-con like Charles Colson, who served time for his part in the Watergate scandal during President Nixon's term of office. He worked with prisoners and ex-cons after his release. A person who suffered from a particular disease now counsels others with that disease. F____'s story, for instance: "My life for 36 years was in complete bondage from alcohol and drugs and of course the struggle got harder and harder as the disease progressed. In 2009 was the darkest day and I hit my knees and cried out to God in surrender. Since then I have been involved in AA and Celebrate Recovery. Today I am grateful for all those years of hell as I know God's purpose for me is to share my experience, strength and hope with those who are still struggling. God can take a mess and turn it into a message and He can take a test and turn it into a testimony. Grateful!"

Or here is T____'s story: "My walk out of 'Egypt' briefly entails what the Lord delivered me from…alcoholism. At 39 I quit wandering around in the wilderness… I was involved in a motor vehicle accident which forever changed my life. I was facing three felony charges which I was innocent of, BUT I had to fight these charges…I always remember what Moses endured and I knew my life was also based on that. God performed a miracle: the charges were dismissed! After three years of being away from my family I finally went home. Today, I've been sober for five years, serve in jail/prison ministry, and thank the Lord for saving me!!"

Each "wounded healer," now redeemed, finds a calling to serve others in the same situation. He understands the language and the challenges. He/she has compassion for others suffering the same difficulties. They recognize the traps, the way we try to weasel out of confronting ourselves. It is a win-win situation for the former addict or ex-con redeeming his/her own life as he/she offers love and support to others. The lessons we learned from the main challenges in our lives become our gift to others suffering from the same thing.

Reading all these stories I have tears in my eyes for the pain and suffering people have had to go through and for how redemptive and life-giving is God's intervention! Here's another one that affected me: V____'s. She was a longtime intravenous drug user in her forties. "In desperation from the misery I cried out to God." All she could say to God was, "Help me, Lord!...But He heard my cry, and I felt Him breaking the chains right then at that moment...at the time I didn't realize what it was I was feeling and hearing...I felt electricity...I heard rattling like chains...the electricity went through my body and out my toes and fingertips." She asked two family members for help. She had one short relapse, before entering a detox program, then called the one person whose phone number she remembered—someone she used to use with who now ran a faith-based recovery home. Today, she cooks dinner for the church on Wednesday nights and for the Celebrate Recovery Program in her church on Sunday nights. She is a leader in that ministry and a certified peer support specialist, visits that recovery home and has started a ministry in jails, on the streets, at homeless camps, helps get people into rehab and meets the needs of anyone she can.

Sometimes it is just simple choices that lead to knowing one's purpose. A woman, J____, was led to a new church by another woman whom she never saw again; she's convinced that she was an angel! The new preacher whom she first saw sweeping the parking lot welcomed her and preached in a way that made the Gospel so relevant to her. "I was so much on fire for the Lord I joined the Jail Ministry and went to the jail to minister hope in Jesus. I opened the doors of my home to the people that were getting out of jail housing them until I could get them into a Christian rehab." She sent a relative to a Christian rehab. He was very reluctant, but is now ordained and in prison ministry himself. She continues, "Now I have met and continue to meet great people that have turned their lives around by the grace of God by His mercy and bringing families together with His love."

Our purpose can be a job, too. Here is D____'s story: "I want to share something about letting God lead you. When I get overwhelmed with too many things to do in too little time, mainly cleaning the house for people coming over, I have anxiety and then I just literally let the Lord lead me all over the house and everything becomes enjoyable, easy and my anxiety disappears and I am in His peace....Also this is kind of different because it's not really the type of godly 'purpose' most people hope to get, but when I got saved I was so in love and 'on fire' for Him and of course, I hoped God would give me this awesome purpose, but I thought about it and was surprised [by] what came out of my mouth to a friend at age 20. I said, 'You know, I don't care if I end up just being a waitress all my life as long as inside my heart and soul I am always serving God.' I said it kind of jokingly, but it must've been a kind of prophecy because now at age 40 I have been waitressing most of the time. I love waitressing and although it's not a purpose that most people would typically hope for, I know who I am on the inside and am okay with it."

I had no intention of being a writer, no obvious talent. But the one thing my life has pointed towards since I surrendered my life to God was figuring out how to be faithful to God, to offer up all that stood between us, to heal the damage the hell-fire-and-damnation-church of my childhood did to me, to bring my whole self before Him (still working on this!). In the late 90's I became a spiritual director accompanying others on their spiritual journeys. After my husband died, one of the things the Lord suggested to me was to take Spanish lessons. As I worked with a tutor she asked me to write paragraphs in Spanish each week. At first I wrote about anything and everything in my life, but later on, all I wanted to write about was living the life centered in God.

Four or five years later, as I moved to Charlotte from California in 2008, I started a bilingual blog writing about the spiritual life and how to lead it in Spanish and English. My tutor was my editor in Spanish. Later that year she was injured in a fall and could no longer help me, so I dropped the Spanish blog. And then in 2011, I committed to posting a blog every Monday and am still doing that to this day. Then I wrote a book on the Kingdom of God and now one on the Exodus story. All because I took the Spanish lessons God suggested! And all because it had taken me years to figure out how to love God and what living the life-with-God entailed.

I don't think writing is the end of the story for me. In fact, I have no idea what the Lord has in mind for me after I complete this book, but I am sure that He will continue to use me in some way for His purposes. Two dreams clarified my purpose for me. In the first one I was talking to the minister of the last church I belonged to in California. I was telling him, "Your job is to inspire the congregation; mine is to connect the dots." As I pondered that dream, it came to me that I was to connect Jesus' teachings with 21st century life. Six months later, I wrote this sentence down in the middle of the night: "to make the Kingdom visible."

Sometimes it seems as if events conspire to reveal a purpose. That was certainly G____'s experience: Her place of employment had just offered her a retirement package which she had taken at age 57. Her company had only done that once in their entire existence. About the same time her daughter's boyfriend became the sole custodian of his three children, aged 6, 7, and 9. He and her daughter married, but both had to work, so G____ stepped into the breech. "We [my husband and I] got the children in school, and I took them and picked them up. I went to their home every day to wash, clean and cook. It wasn't easy taking care of three children who I was a stranger to. I bought them clothes, food and helped to supply their needs financially. My husband and I saw that those children never went without anything.

Now they are all grown and they are truly our grandchildren. We are proud of them. One of the boys is going to school to be a doctor; he sent me a little note telling me how grateful he was for everything I had done for him. The other boy works with UPS, and the girl has been married and has two little girls that we adore. We have had to again help her along the way as her husband abandoned her and the children. These children that I took under my wing have truly become my family. It was hard at times, but I am so grateful I was there to lend a hand when there was no one else to help these precious children. I thank God that He gave me the strength and the finances to be there for them. Had I not received that early retirement package, I would not have been able to be there to help raise them and help their dad financially. God truly works in mysterious ways!!

As I wrote at the beginning of this section on purpose, to advance His Kingdom on Earth is the general purpose He has for all of us. How we do that depends on our gifts and talent, and the challenges we faced in this lifetime. Everyone has a purpose, an important one. It doesn't matter who you are, how educated you are, what race you are—nothing matters except that you love God and want to follow God and to fulfill your purpose here. You see, in the Kingdom of God, everyone is essential and the only person who stands above anyone else is Christ Himself. And in the Kingdom, which forms a true community of people who live their beliefs and who serve God, everyone is valued by everyone else. We'll talk more about the Kingdom of God in Part IV.

The laws handed down in the second half of the wilderness story are symbolic of the way God will come into our lives to help us live out our purpose in the spirit of the law and commandments. He will train and instruct, heal and transform all areas of non-compliance; He will highlight our challenges and attachments. He will do this in every aspect of our lives, if we will let Him in—in our jobs, in our relationships, in our leisure, in our worship, in our deepest pain and suffering. As we are destined to co-partnership[149] with God in all areas of our lives, He will want our agreement in everything and, especially, in the laying aside of all rebellion. All this is the potential within us until we are serious about this relationship. Only God can bring us to the realization of who we were created to be and whose we are.

Then God will also reveal to us what our purpose is. As the stories I've quoted above indicate, "there are different kinds of gifts, but the same Spirit distributes them. There are different kinds of service, but the same Lord. There are different kinds of working, but in all of them in everyone it is the same God at work."[150] Each person's gifts and purpose are used to the glory of God and to the visibility of the Kingdom of God on Earth. Each has the same value. God has entrusted our purpose to each of us, so that when we have

---

[149] More about this in Part IV Chapter 2
[150] 1 Corinthians 12:4-6

the right relationship to Him, we will be ready to give back those very gifts to God. "We have different gifts, according to the grace given to each of us. If your gift is prophesying, then prophesy in accordance with your faith; if it is serving, then serve; if it is teaching, then teach; if it is to encourage, then give encouragement; if it is giving, then give generously; if it is to lead, do it diligently; if it is to show mercy, do it cheerfully."[151]

God

God is still highly visible to the Israelites in the second part of the wilderness story after the debacle of Ba'al. He can be seen in a cloud over the Tent of Meeting by day and a pillar of fire by night. After Moses spent a second forty days on Mount Sinai with the Lord, returning with the second tablet of the Ten Commandments, he met regularly with God in the Tent of Meeting. And while Moses met with God, all the people stood at the entrance of their own tents in worship, too.[152] Moses' face would be so glowing after their meeting that he wore a veil when he left the tent,[153] so as not to overwhelm the people who encountered him. Moses was in the stage of *illumination.*

As long as the pillar of cloud rested above the tent, the people stayed in place. When the cloud moved away, the people got ready to move. God was leading them through the wilderness; they were wandering until they would be ready to follow Him--without rebellion--into the Promised

---

[151] Romans 12:6-8
[152] Exodus 33:7-11
[153] Exodus 34:29-35

Land. And He was seeing to their needs—for nourishment, for work, for their spirit.

God began to organize the tribes for the traveling and eventual takeover of Canaan, i.e. setting the positions of the tribes in the various camps and for worship. He ordered a census of each tribe. He bestowed on some individuals, Bezalel and Oholiab, for example, the skills and the wisdom they would need to oversee the construction of all the elements of the Tabernacle and the Ark, the materials used in it, for example, everything from the altar of wood to the garments made of weavings.[154]

He named Aaron and his sons, priests to the Israelites.[155] Then appointed the tribe of Levi to assist the priests. And even gave three clans of the Levites special duties in assisting the priests as detailed in the previous chapter.

He reiterated and expanded on the Ten Commandments so that, ". . . you may fear the Lord your God as long as you live by keeping all his decrees and commands that I give you...be careful to obey so that it may go well with you and that you may increase greatly in a land flowing with mild and honey, just as the Lord, the God of your ancestors promised you."[156] He declares Himself the only God, "the Lord is one."[157] And He enjoined them to, ". . .

---

[154] Exodus 31:1-11
[155] Numbers 3:2-4
[156] Deuteronomy 6:2-3
[157] Deuteronomy 6:4

.. not forget the Lord who brought you out of Egypt, out of the land of slavery."[158]

He described himself as a jealous God whose "anger will burn against you, and he will destroy you from the face of the land. Do not put the Lord your God to the test as you did at Massah"[159] [where they complained about the lack of water]. He set out laws about offerings[160] and detailed the duties and garments of the priests[161] and all the parts of the Tabernacle and Ark.[162]

He laid down laws about tithing, giving Him the first fruits of their harvests.[163] There were laws about different kinds of offerings—burnt, grain, drink, fellowship, freewill, sin, guilt, supplementary, and unintentional sins.[164] He named the festivals they were to celebrate and when: Passover, Sabbath, Weeks, Tabernacles Trumpets, Day of Atonement.[165] He was very concerned about the purity of the camps and handed down laws about that, laws about defiling skin diseases and molds, about when, after a woman gave birth or menstruated, she could be ritually cleansed.[166]

He granted the Reubenites, the Gadites and one-half the tribe of Manasseh land on the wilderness or East side of

---

[158] Deuteronomy 6:12
[159] Deuteronomy 6:15-16
[160] Leviticus 1:2-17 for example
[161] Exodus 39:1 for example
[162] Exodus 36:8-38 for example
[163] Leviticus 27:30-32 for example
[164] i.e. Exodus 35:29, 40:29, Numbers 6:15, Leviticus 7:34, 35, 4:13-14, 4:27-31
[165] Leviticus 23
[166] Leviticus 13, Leviticus 12:4-6

the River Jordan as they requested because it was "suitable for livestock."[167] And the men of these tribes in return would help the rest of the Israelites conquer Canaan.

And the Lord showed the Israelites what would happen when they went out on their own and when they followed His lead in dealing with their enemies. When the scouts came back from their mission to assess the challenges in Canaan, they reported untruthfully about the size and fierceness of the various peoples there. Only Joshua and Caleb told the truth.[168] The whole nation was up in arms and set out to attack the Amalekites and Canaanites who lived in the hill country. Although Moses warned them that they would be unsuccessful without God's blessing and leadership, they attacked anyway and were roundly defeated.

But when God led them against Sihon and Og, for example, they conquered them.[169] Then he taught them how to deal with the conquered peoples and their territory.[170]

Perhaps the most powerful teaching of this wilderness story is about the blessings that will be theirs if the Israelites obey God and the curses that will accrue if they are not obedient. "This day I call the heavens and the earth as witness against you that I have set before you life and death, blessings and curses. Now choose life, so that you and

---

[167] Numbers 32
[168] Deuteronomy 1:19-46
[169] Deuteronomy 21:21-35
[170] Deuteronomy 2:31-37

your children may live and that you may love the Lord your God, listen to his voice and hold fast to him."[171]

In summarizing this part of the Exodus story and God's part in it, we could say that God is highly visible. That He began organizing the lives of the Israelites, defining each one's purpose and giving them the skills to do what He needed them to do. He assigned priests for the people and support for the priests. He commented on and expanded the Ten Commandments, extending their reach to every aspect of the life in the camps and by extension in the Promised Land to come. He talked about being a jealous God, wishing to be the only God the Israelites worshiped. He described their worship, tithing, and festivals. He was concerned about the purity of the camp, about any attempt to worship other gods.

He demonstrated to them what happened when they went off on their own to fight their enemies and when they followed His initiative. In the first place they were defeated; with Him leading, they were successful. And He taught that as long as they followed His laws, they would be blessed and if they didn't, they would be cursed. He supported, sustained and led them through all the trials of the wilderness. He fulfilled His promises.

God was busily training the Israelites so they would be ready to enter the Promised Land obedient to Him and ready to take over the land at His direction. He is willing to wait forty years in the wilderness until the generation He brought out of Egypt have died off, because they are too rebellious, too attached to going back. The wilderness where

---

[171]Deuteronomy 30:19-20

we find ourselves, plucked of our normal lives, is a place where He has our attention, where we are more dependent on Him, where we suffer from being in unfamiliar territory—there God can speak to us and we are more apt to hear Him.

Now the people that He originally led out of Egypt have not been able to leave behind the past; they were still longing to return to the white-washed memories of the past. But the wisdom of the wilderness is that we have to leave the past behind. And when we are able to do that, we see God and ourselves in a whole new light. As William Clemmons, a professor of theology towards the end of the 20th century, wrote, "God's activity goes on all around us and we are tragically unaware of it."

What a great difference it would be for us if we could see the traces of God in our lives, His ever-present help and support, the blessings and grace He showers on us, the suggestions from Him that might come through any one we meet or from the "still, small voice" within us of 1 Kings 19:12. Instead, we are like the Israelites complaining because God isn't doing what we want done in our lives. He's doing the things that would help us the most, that would bring us to wholeness, to fulfillment, to our purpose, but we can't see His presence and actions all around us.

We're still committed to seeing everything through the cultural lens and our own personal lens, and often, we don't like what we see. Or we pray for a particular outcome and are disappointed that God didn't answer our prayer. Instead, we could ponder why He didn't want that choice for us and what He did send instead. Perhaps He objected to our ego-centered choice, which would do nothing to bring us closer to Him and to our own true selves.

So, whether we've lost our job or a loved one, whether we have finally faced our addictions, whether we have an illness, we're newly divorced or suffered the loss of our home, or we've given our lives over to God-- no matter what brought us out into the wilderness, we can see God more easily here than when we're in the "real world."All we have to do is to turn our attention on Him. These are the things that God wants us to hear. 1) How to organize our lives. 2) What our purpose is. 3) How to be holy in His eyes. 4) What His laws are. 5) How to worship Him. 6) Who He is to be to us. 7) How to follow His leadings. 8) How to depend on Him day and night. 9) How to follow Him in everything we do. This second stage of the wilderness is an in-depth course for each of us in how to be with God. This is the purpose of the wilderness—for us to come into a deep and dependent relationship with God, for us to become a partner of God in all our endeavors, for us to follow His leadings. And when we have finally given up all rebellion against God, all attachment to our own very human ways of being and thinking, then we are finally camped on the banks of the River Jordan where we will once again cross holy waters.

Now in the stage of *Illumination* we can see ourselves and God clearly. And we are being readied to move into the state of *Union*. In crossing the Red Sea it was our initial baptism, that born-again moment or a moment of surrendering our lives to God, which propelled us into the wilderness by saying that first "yes!" to following God. Or we may have arrived in the wilderness through a traumatic event. Either way, at some point we have decided to follow

God. Now, at the end of traveling in the wilderness, in crossing the Jordan, we will be baptized of the Holy Spirit, the blessing of Pentecost, the ascendency of the Indwelling Spirit of God within us. It is in that state of being wholly in the Spirit of God that is necessary before we enter Canaan or the Kingdom of God.

There are many lessons for us in how the Israelites rebelled and complained all along the way in the wilderness. We, too, grumble when what is happening in our lives is not what we wanted. We, too, experience the dislocation of the wilderness and resent our having to be there. We, rebellious human beings that we are, want to exercise our free will, to make things the way we like them to be. Our ideas are all based on what the world taught us to want. We resent God for not answering our prayers immediately and in the manner we desire. We even take it personally if He rejects our desires. We object to the suffering we see everywhere, especially our own.

Jean-Pierre de Caussade, an 18th century Jesuit, would upend our understanding of suffering: "to live by faith, then, is to live in joy, confidence, certainty and trust in all there is to do and suffer each moment as ordained by God. However mysterious it may seem, it is in order to awaken and maintain this living faith that God drags the soul through tumultuous floods of so much suffering, trouble, perplexity, weariness and ruin."[172]

---

[172] Jean-Pierre de Caussade, *The Sacrament of the Present Moment,* English translation by William Collins Sons & Co., HarperOne, New York, 1981, p. 22

All this rebelliousness has to die off or be healed before we can really come before God in love with all of ourselves. There is no way we can hide our negativity from God; there is no way we can hide our guilt and shame from Him. All we can do is to look that rebelliousness in the eye and accept it for what it is—part of our world-centered, ego-centered ways. The energy that we expend in resisting what comes into our lives can be better spent in adjusting to the reality in them, in aligning ourselves with God's will.

I do believe that we create a great deal of our own pain and suffering by resisting what we don't like in our lives. And our resistance multiplies the suffering we experience. It's not that we don't sometimes have to adjust our thinking to accept some new thing that has come into our lives. But we are far happier if we not only just accept it, but also are grateful for all that we are given. We could change our attitude from resisting what is already in our life to looking for the core of what we are to learn from having this thing in our lives. It is a shift from the world's perspective to God's perspective.

We have this nonsensical idea that we should not have to suffer, that we should have a painless existence. But that is not what God promises us. He promises us that He will take care of us, meet our needs, walk alongside us in whatever happens to us. But a pain-free existence? No!

This is the great saga of the wilderness: to go from a world-centered existence, leaving all that behind, in order to follow God willingly wherever He would take us. To give up our own ways and to adopt God's ways. To stop going off on our own and to just live in God's will.

All this time from Egypt through the wilderness the Israelites have followed God's leadings with Moses being his spokesman, even as they rebelled against Him. But in the aftermath of the scouts' report from Canaan and the death of those who lied, the Israelites set out the next morning to take Canaan. Moses cried out to them, "Why are you disobeying the Lord's command? This will not succeed! Do not go up, because the Lord is not with you. You will be defeated by your enemies." Nevertheless, the Israelites went to the highest point in the hill country, ". . . though neither Moses nor the ark of the Lord's covenant moved from the camp." And they were defeated.[173]

God desires a partnership with us, wherein we follow His directions, wait for His leading, as I found out in trying to write this book the first time, it was a no-go when I was working in my own way with my own sense of timing. I had to follow His ways, His timing. In God's eyes, timing and following His lead are probably the most important consideration in all that we do. If we go out on our own too early or two late, we will not be successful. If we don't follow His lead, we will not be successful. But at the right time and in the right place, doing what we were shown to do, our task will be done effortlessly.

This is a difficult thing for us. We have our own way of doing things and we like to do them that way, whether it has been successful for us or not. I like to push through all obstacles and make things happen. That is our cultural, our American way --"making things happen." We are not trained to wait for the right timing, to follow God's leadings. Even in churches, we often are just following the culture or

---

[173] Numbers 14:40-46

the world's way of doing things. For instance, there is a big idea out there that we are to grow our congregation's size. Adding more Christians is the obvious reason, but often it is about filling our coffers, showing how successful we as a church are. It has little to do with gathering people whose lives are changed by coming into God's house.

Is there any credence given to listening for God's take on this? Or do we follow a corporate model of how to grow the size? How many churches pray for guidance, wait for the Lord's leadings, even ask what He wants done here and now? Or do we just offer a prayer for guidance at the beginning of the meeting and then forget about God in our decisions?

The lesson that God is trying to promote to us is simply this: Obey Me, listen to Me, follow Me and you will be blessed. Our rebelliousness is the major wall between us and God. You may have noticed that every time the Israelites rebelled against God, they died. I take this as a metaphor: that the rebellion has to go. It has to die out. It has to be absorbed into the deeper direction of the soul. The ego, the rebellious part of us, has to come under the aegis of the soul.

I cannot emphasize enough that God is not a bigger version of a human being, sitting up in His chariot in the sky with a thunderbolt in His hand ready to zap us or bless us. God is beyond gender and human form. He is our Creator and Sustainer. He is Mystery itself. He is Love. As the head of the Trinity, He relies greatly on His Son and Spirit to be with us at all times, in all places.

We humans tend to humanize God, to see Him as the big parent in the sky. And I can see how we get there from some of these Exodus texts. But, unlike us, God adheres to His laws. He sometimes is angry or disappointed in the Israelites, but He is Love Himself. He cannot be seen, but He can be experienced. The more faithful we have been to Him, the more we build our own body of experience of God in each of us. This is more important than any belief you have about God, because when we have the experience of God, we know Him deeply inside ourselves. It's not someone else telling us about God or even reading about Him in the Old and New Testaments. What we know and have experienced can never be taken from us. It remains a part of us, incontestable. Our experience of God is God telling us Who He is.

God is God and cannot be changed by us. The best we can do is to follow where He leads, to be in constant contact, to love Him with all of ourselves. And then we are changed into the people He created us to be.

Illumination

Remember, we are looking at the Exodus story as a template for how we get back to that deep relationship with God, to where we can live in the Kingdom. Even as God is readying the Israelites to cross the River Jordan into the Promised Land, He is predicting the difficulty the Israelites will have with the new land. God is predicting to Moses just before He dies that, "These people will soon prostitute themselves to the foreign gods of the land they are entering. They will forsake me and break the covenant I made with them. And in that day I will become angry with them and forsake them." He goes on to predict that many disasters will visit them. And that God will hide His face from them.[174]

By this time in the wilderness, after all the Israelites have been through and have come to be obedient to God, I think that God is saying this: "By this time you should never again miss the mark of what I am asking you to do. By this time there should just be obedience. Here in the stage of *illumination*: There should no longer be any rebellion, there should only be the desire to think like I think and do what I ask you to do." In the illumination stage, one "has now got through preliminaries; detached himself from his chief entanglements; re-oriented his instinctive life. The result is a new and solid certitude about God, and his own soul's relation to God: an 'enlightenment' in which he is adjusted to new standards of conduct and thought...he is 'proficient' but not yet perfect."[175]

I think that we could look at Moses and Aaron as two men of the old order who have done their jobs really well (with a couple of lapses for both) until now. They have gone as far as they can go with God, because there is still something in them that lives in the world itself, which will never convert totally to God's ways.

So Aaron, 123 years old, dies at Meribah and Moses will die at Mount Nebo, which is just east of the Jordan River. It will take a leader who has never rebelled, who has no connection to Egypt/to the world who will lead them into the Promised Land. So Moses, who has been so incredibly

---

[174] Deuteronomy 31:16-18
[175] Evelyn Underhill, *Mysticism:A study in the Nature and Development of Spiritual Consciousness*, Dover Publications, Mineola NY, 2002p. 234

faithful and now so old at 120 years, died and the Lord appointed Joshua as his replacement.

As we will see in Part IV in the Book of Joshua, God has found someone who is in perfect rhythm with Him, who obeys, who is at one with the Lord—Joshua himself. This is *Union* the fourth state of the spiritual journey. Joshua is that part of us that has come forward in us through the stages of awakening, purgation and illumination. Our inner Joshua, in each of us, tells the truth, listens to and is obedient to the Lord *always*. He is the one who can lead us into the Kingdom, into the Promised Land. He takes the torch from Moses and represents God to us in all that we do. He and his lieutenant, Caleb, have never been touched by rebellion, have never strayed. They are the human being raised to a different level of being in God.

It seems to me that God needs a secure footing within us in order to communicate fully to us His plans, what we should say and do, where we should go. Where Moses was an inner bridge to the soul and could hear the voice of the Indwelling Spirit of God, Joshua represents the soul fully in its total devotion to God.

Patricia Said Adams

Part III: From Egypt to Freedom

Chapter Five

Conclusions

Part III of the Exodus story is a complex story of the Israelites representing us, of God, and of the wilderness. The purpose of the wilderness is to isolate us from the world's influence and to provide little distraction from the relationship with God, so that we can process out of us all the very human stuff we carry—leftovers of pain and suffering, wounds from the past, even our very own selves, especially our own self-image which is usually very negative, so that we can come into the present with God, into His presence, unburdened by anything that went before. This is a long process for us of owning the contents of our conscious and unconscious minds. Referring back to the symbol of the iceberg, all that is in us, conscious (1/7 above the surface of the sea) and unconscious (beneath the surface) is to gradually melt into the vast fullness and emptiness of the sea who is God. We are to become one with the Source of all creation, to act in His will and with His love in everything we do. This is the potential that God holds out to all of us once the rebellion, the free will, the ego-centeredness, the world-dominated in us is gone, or rather has been brought under the aegis of the soul.

God's main teaching vehicle is the Law, the letter of the Law and the Spirit of the Law which is summarized in Jesus' Two Great Commandments: "Love the Lord your God with all your heart and with all your soul and with all your mind…[and] Love our neighbor as yourself."[176] Here is Pastor Steve Garnass-Holmes' take on the meaning of the commandments to love God:

"The command to love God is first

not simply because it's the most important,

but because it's the only commandment.

God is One; God is the only one; God is all.

How we do anything is how we love God.

How we love a neighbor, love a stranger,

love an enemy, this is our love of God.

How we eat our food or notice beauty,

how we express gratitude, treat mistakes,

trust grace, offer gifts, be patient or forgive

---

[176] Matthew 22:37-40; Mark 12:29-31 and Luke 10:27 both add "and with all your strength."

is how we love God.

Our tenderness or harshness

toward the ugly and the disturbing,

our acceptance of pleasure and torment,

our longing for wholeness,

our hunger for love,

our longing for God,

is how we love God.

Our sitting and listening,

our growing and being,

our breathing,

is how we love God.

*

O Love,

perfect your love in us."[177]

Loving God is everything. We show how we love God by how we do everything, especially by how we treat ourselves and all our neighbors.

In Old Testament terms once we comply with the first four Commandments, once the rebellion is over, then we

---

[177] Rev. Steve Garnaas-Holmes' daily email of 10.28.15. www.unfoldinglight.net

find ourselves in God's arms, no longer able to do anything but to follow Him. We don't even have to know the details of the Law, for we are no longer letter-of-the-law people; we would no longer do anything against the One we love. We live in the arms of Love, Compassion, Mercy and Justice and that is who we are, too. This is what it means to live in the Kingdom of God here on Earth. And we will find more detail about this in Part IV.

Meanwhile we have gone through the stages of *Awakening, Purgation* and *Illumination.* We have shed all the rebellion and have totally aligned our own will with God's. Parts of us just had to die off; other parts got healed, transformed and incorporated in us, adding to our ability to love and to follow. Just as the Israelites finally stopped rebelling after the incidents with the snakes[178] and the Moabite women,[179] so we can finally align our will with God's will. Even God's appointed leader, Moses, who led us to this place at the banks of the River Jordan has died. All the Israelites who first left "Egypt" have died off. Moses' work is done; he dies and Joshua takes over as God's leader/spokesman role in us. Joshua is that part of us that has never rebelled, never seen himself as distinct from God.

We have found our purpose. God has revealed it to us: to bring in the Kingdom of God in our own unique way. So now our talents and gifts and the lessons we have learned from the pain and suffering we have experienced translate into the way, our own unique way, of bringing in the Kingdom.

---

[178] Numbers 21:4-8
[179] Numbers 25

The whole wilderness experience is the template which prepares us for the fourth step: Baptism by the Holy Spirit as we cross the River Jordan into the Promised Land, into the Kingdom of God. Then, like Paul and the Disciples, we are one with God, one with His will, one with what He wants us to say and do, one with whatever happens whether it is joy-filled or horror-filled. This passage in the wilderness is the most significant one of our lives, because we are truly leaving behind the ways of the world, the thinking of the world and our own self-absorption, even if that self-absorption is in God.

Patricia Said Adams

Part IV: The Promised Land

Chapter One

Introduction, The Israelites

Part IV Covers the entire Book of Joshua

Introduction to Part IV: Union with God, Living in the Kingdom

The Book of Joshua opens on the eastern banks of the Jordan River where the Israelites have camped before entering the Promised Land, Canaan. They are at the end of the wilderness journey of forty years, done with the purging of all the rebelliousness that would separate them from God. They are now in the third stage—*illumination*—of the spiritual journey, seeing life and God clearly for the first time. They are obedient, no longer out of duty but out of love for God, ready to follow God's lead in moving into the territory that God has promised Abraham and all his progeny-- Canaan will be their new home. They are unencumbered by the burden of their parents' attachment to Egypt. They have been formed by the forty years in the wilderness, stripped of all worldly concerns and anticipating finding a home at last in the rich land that is Canaan. Their focus is on listening to God through His newly-appointed spokesman, Joshua.

Each person now is responsible for believing in God and in listening to God, the power in the religion is in each one of them, collectively as the nation of Israel. It is not just an inherited communal religion now; it is a hard-won, individually-based response to God in a community of believers. But it is more than just belief: These Israelites know God. They know His scriptures. They have lived His promises in the wilderness and not only survived the wilderness, but have come close to God through all the challenges and suffering. They know who they are and what they are to do. And they are ready to get beyond the conquering of Canaan into settling into their new, permanent home.

Union is the last stage of the spiritual life; it initiates us into that close partnership with God, where we no longer know the source of how we think, whether it is God or ourselves; it just doesn't matter. It starts with the baptism of the Holy Spirit when the Indwelling Spirit of God comes to the fore in us as the primary source of power and personality. Union with God is "a definite state or form of enhanced life. It is obtained neither from an intellectual realization of its delights, nor from the most acute emotional longings. Though these must be present, they are not enough. It is arrived at by an arduous psychological and spiritual process...entailing the complete remaking of character and the liberation of a new, or rather latent, form of consciousness."[180]

This is a stage far beyond where most of us would think was the end of the journey with God here on Earth, but there are many writings of the Apostle Paul and the saints who describe what it is like, for example, to still be Paul of Tarsus or Teresa of Avila and to be living with God so intimately. His epistles are filled with his experience: for example, when the ship he was imprisoned on was about to crash into land during a storm. He prays, he gives thanks, he insists the sailors eat ...[181] Teresa of Avila's autobiography is filled with stories of living a life in God.[182]

Perhaps the most telling example of union with God in the Bible is with Abraham who was willing to place his precious son Isaac on the altar as God has commanded him in Genesis 22. When Isaac asked his father where the lamb for the sacrifice was, Abraham told him that God would provide. Abraham tied Isaac to the altar on top of the wood; he was about to take a knife to his son, when God intervened. And nearby there was a ram for the sacrifice.[183] It was the absolute trust in God that Abraham exhibited in this story that prompted God to promise him as many descendants as the stars.

---

[180] Evelyn Underhill, *Mysticism: A study in the Nature and Development of Spiritual Consciousness*, Dover Publications, Mineola, New York, 2002, p. 81
[181] Acts 27:27-28:6
[182] *Teresa of Avila: The Book of My Life* or similar title, *The Life of St. Teresa of Jesus*
[183] Genesis 22:1-18

Here is how one of my readers, C_____, described being filled with the Holy Spirit: "My Grandmother was a pastor before there were many female pastors, so needless to say I was blessed to be reared in a Christian home. I gave my life to God as a child like many, but I am a true testimony of what you call a time of waiting between true surrender and Holy Spirit filling. I will never forget that moment in high school during a revival that the Lord spoke to me in the only the [way] He can! I was laid out in the Spirit and began to speak in tongues for the very first time. Needless to say that single experience changed my life forever!!! I am now 57 and Spirit filled for forty years!"

The Promised Land is not without challenges; there are entrenched interests that the Israelites have to conquer. There are gods and practices to avoid, artifacts and devoted things to destroy. There is the absolute trust in the Israelites in God and the willingness to follow Him wherever He leads. God is there; He has a plan that works for each challenge. And each challenge took a new approach, so they were not to assume that after Jericho, for example, was conquered,[184] that every other challenge would be met in the same way. They must be prepared to continue to listen to God in all things, to heed His advice in each instance, to continue to follow His lead, to be obedient.

They no longer are to go off on their own, to rebel. That is one of the big things they have given up in the wilderness, because they have not been successful at all every time they tried.

---

[184] Joshua 5:13-6:27

Eagerness would be one way to describe the Israelites as they prepare to cross the Jordan. They are about to leave the wilderness having integrated the lessons learned there. They are to move in and conquer Canaan, a rich land in which they will thrive. The minute that they taste of the bounty of the land, manna disappears![185] Confidence and trust in God thrive: God has brought them out of the long sojourn in the wilderness. They know He will keep His promises. Open to what happens and trusting in Him is another way of expressing their confidence in Him. And ready to face the challenges ahead with God leading, remembering their successes with Him, their failures without God.

God

And what is God doing in the Book of Joshua? God is showing the Israelites how He keeps His promises, how He fulfills His covenants with them. While the wilderness was a time of preparation and healing and transformation, the "Promised Land" is the gift that God is giving, as He promised, to the descendants of Abraham and Isaac. He is "a covenant-keeping and a promise-keeping God!"[186], the One we can count on above all else. He stops the manna that He has produced six days a week for forty years as soon as the Israelites taste the bounty of the land of Canaan.

And He leads the Israelites into battle against all the kingdoms of Canaan. God shows us the range of His tactics in conquering Canaan through Jericho and all the other

---

[185] Joshua 5:12

[186] John D. Currid, *Strong and Courageous: Joshua Simply Explained*, EP Books, Carlisle PA, 2011, p. 198

kingdoms of the territory. It matters not whether it is a one-city kingdom as in Ai or whether five kingdoms are banded together to fight the Israelites. God's people are victorious, because they follow His lead.

As they are about to cross the River Jordan, God asks the Israelites to follow the Ark of the Covenant held by the priests across the River Jordan into the Promised Land. He asks only that they be obedient and worship only Him.

And so, with God leading and the Israelites following, they are successful over the years in taking over the territory that He promised them; they defeat the Sihon, king of the Amorites, and Og, king of the Bashan, plus twenty-nine other kings. There were still some kings in power at the end of Joshua's life that would have to be dealt with, but in the meantime God asked that the territories be divided among the tribes of Israel.

Joshua and the Israelites

Joshua is the main character of Part IV of the Exodus story, just as Moses was of the first three parts. Where Moses was God's spokesman and leader, Joshua is spokesman and leader *and* a warrior, ready to lead the Israelites in conquering the Promised Land. He has never failed to follow God's orders, never rebelled against them.

Moses died just this side of the Jordan River at Mount Nebo. He was an old man who was not to see the Promised Land. He had disobeyed God once and was not to see what God had promised the Israelites since Abraham's time.[187]

---

[187]Numbers 20:8, 11

Also he was identified with the whole process of leaving Egypt and all the rebellion in the wilderness. He certainly did a great job as God's spokesman and leader of the Israelites through the forty plus years of the wilderness. But the Israelites were to take a new leader, one who had never rebelled against God, to lead the Israelites into Canaan. Joshua was clear about who was in charge and what his role was to be. And he was a warrior, the leader needed to fight off all the nations they would have to unseat in Canaan.

Joshua was installed as leader of the Israelites with this charge from God:

"Moses my servant is dead. Now then, you and all these people, get ready to cross the Jordan River into the land I am about to give to them—to the Israelites. I will give you every place where you set your foot, as I promised Moses. Your territory will extend from the desert to Lebanon, and from the great river, the Euphrates—all the Hittite country—to the Mediterranean Sea in the west. No one will be able to stand against you all the days of your life. As I was with Moses, so I will be with you; I will never leave you nor forsake you. Be strong and courageous, because you will lead these people to inherit the land I swore to their ancestors to give them.

"Be strong and very courageous. Be careful to obey all the law my servant Moses gave you; do not turn from it to the right or to the left, that you may be successful wherever you go. Keep this Book of the Law always on your lips; meditate on it day and night, so that you may be careful to do everything written in it. Then you will be prosperous and successful. Have I not commanded you? Be strong and courageous. Do not be afraid; do not be discouraged, for the Lord your God will be with you wherever you go."[188]

Joshua is not only the leader who has never rebelled, but the people that he leads, too, have not rebelled against God. They are descendants of the generation that God led out of slavery; they are not their rebellious parents who had never let go of their dream of returning to Egypt.

The Israelites are to follow the priests carrying the Ark of the Covenant into the Jordan River at a little distance behind them and then to walk past the priests to the other bank. And so, the whole nation of Israelites crossed the Jordan.

After crossing into Canaan one man from each tribe was to pick a stone from the dry river bed to create a memorial that celebrated the crossing of the River Jordan because God had cut off the flood waters above to create a passageway in which the priests held the Ark of the Covenant until all the Israelites had passed. Then the priests, too, climbed the far banks of the Jordan and joined the rest of the Israelites. As they left the river bed, the flood-stage waters of the Jordan River returned.

Then God ordered Joshua to make flint knives and to circumcise all the men of the tribes of Israel.[189] Circumcision is a sign of the covenant with God; it was believed to complete the Hebrew male.[190]

---

[188] Joshua 1:7-9

[189] Joshua 5:2-8 no circumcisions had been done since leaving Egypt.

[190] Genesis 17:9-14, Lev. 12:3

Then they celebrated Passover. They ate some of the produce of the land plus unleavened bread and roasted grain. The manna stopped after this celebration—after sustaining them for forty years.[191]

Joshua led the Israelites in conquering all these kings and peoples and in the distribution of the land. The conquering of Jericho is probably one of the best-known stories of the Old Testament. At least one song has been written about it; the Biblical story has been told to many generations of children. First, two spies are sent out to assess the situation in Jericho and they meet Rahab, a prostitute, who hid the men from the king. In return for her protection she and her family were to be treated kindly, that is, allowed to live, by the Israelites.[192]

It is the first of the city-kingdoms in Canaan that the Israelites conquer and in such a colorful way: six days of circling the city by all the armed men. On the 7th day the Israelites were to "march around the city seven times with the priests blowing the trumpets. When you hear them sound a long blast on the trumpets, have the whole army give a loud shout; then the wall of the city will collapse and the army will go up, everyone straight in."[193] And so it was.

In the aftermath of the taking of Jericho, the subsequent failure against the army of Ai highlights the only incidence of rebellion in the whole book of Joshua. It was called Achan's Sin. The Lord had warned them against taking any of the sacred objects of any of the peoples of

---

[191] Joshua 5:10-12
[192] Joshua 2:1-21
[193] Joshua 6

Canaan,[194] but Achan took some from Jericho. Because of this God's anger prevented the Israelites from being successful against the army of Ai. When Joshua—not knowing that Achan had kept some of the spoils-- complained about the loss, God told him that someone had plundered some of the sacred objects and had to die for it. When Achan confessed, he was stoned, then his whole family was stoned and all their possessions were burned.[195] God had predicted rebellion among His people before they crossed the Jordan.[196] Even with all the gains in abiding with God and letting go of all rebellion, it still occurred.

The story of the successful capture of Jericho spread throughout the land; kings in the hill country, the foothills and along the Mediterranean coast plotted as allies to fight against the Israelites and their God. The Gibeonites, close neighbors of Jericho, decided to head off any capture of their lands. A delegation dressed as if they had been on a long journey. They carried moldy bread and bad food. And when they reached the Israelites, they asked Joshua to make a treaty with them. They deceived him into thinking they lived a long way away. Within three days they Israelites found out that the Gibeonites were close neighbors. The Israelites stuck to the treaty they had innocently made with the Gibeonites, but because of the deception they would have to serve the Israelites as water carriers and woodcutters from then on.[197]

---

[194] Deuteronomy 13:15-17
[195] Joshua 7
[196] Deuteronomy 31:14
[197] Joshua 9

With the sin of Achan behind them and after dealing with the Gibeonites, the Israelites led by Joshua were successful in conquering the many territories of this new land: Sihon, king of the Amorites, Og, king of Bashan, king of Jericho, king of Ai, of Jerusalem, Hebron, Jarmuth, Lachish, Eglon, Gezer, Debir, Geder, Hormah, Arad, Libnah, Adullam, Makkedah, Bethel, Tappuah, Hepher, Aphek, Lasharon, Madon, Hazor, Shimron Meron, Akshaph, Taanach, Megiddo, Kedesh, Jokneam in Carmet, Naphoth Dor, Goyim in Gilgal and Tirzah.[198] There were still a few territories for the Israelites to conquer as Joshua neared the end of his life.

Now the lands were distributed to all the tribes except to the tribe of Levi, "since the food offerings presented to the Lord, the God of Israel, are their inheritance, as he promised them,[199] as well as towns and pasture lands. Towns and cities were set aside for the Levites and Cities of refuge were set up where an accidental murderer could flee and find sanctuary, often in the same towns that were given to the Levites.

After much of Canaan was conquered, each tribe was given a portion of the land. Half of the Manasseh tribe, the Reubenites and the Gadites returned to the inheritance they had already received East of the Jordan River.[200] The tribes of Judah, Ephraim and the other half of the Manassehs were allotted land.[201] Joshua asked the remaining tribes to map out the rest of the land and to divide it into sevenths. Then

---

[198] Joshua 12
[199] Joshua 13:14
[200] Joshua 13:8-13
[201] Joshua 15 & 16

he "cast lots for them in Shiloh in the presence of the Lord, and there he distributed the land to the Israelites according to their tribal divisions."[202]

---

[202] Joshua 18:8-10

Part IV: The Promised Land

Chapter Two

Union with God, Characters, etc.

Union with God

The crossing of the River Jordan is symbolic of the second baptism of our spiritual lives, the entry of the Holy Spirit into leadership over our lives, akin to the Pentecost experience of the Disciples of Jesus. Once we've awaken to our slavery to the world, spent a long time in the wilderness purging ourselves of all that stands between us and God— that personal and cultural lens through which we view everything, has been illumined, healed of all rebellion, so that we can now see how God sees, *then* we are ready for the last stage of the Spiritual Journey in God--*union* with God. It is the goal of all spiritual journeying.

We have to turn to the mystics of our Christian history to understand this stage of the spiritual journey. According to Gerald May, MD and spiritual author, union with God "is neither accomplished on our own nor worked within us by God alone. For Teresa (of Avila) and John (of the Cross), it is a "mystical co-participation between God and the person. With God as the center of the human soul it can be no other way."[203] It is our total willingness, our "soul's free and true yes to God...that God freely and truly gives the yes of divine grace."[204]

There is a seamlessness in the union with God, according to Thomas Merton, a 20th century Trappist monk. "What happens is that the separate entity that is *you* apparently disappears and nothing seems to be left but a pure freedom indistinguishable from infinite Freedom, love identified with Love. Not two loves, one waiting for the other, striving for the other, seeking for the other, but Love Loving in Freedom."[205] There is left in the person little identity in the world.

We can see this oneness in Joshua where God's plan was laid out in every instance and followed exactly. Only once in the whole Book of Joshua do we see any rebellion--in Achan's holding on to sacred things from Jericho. Once Achan's sin was punished, not only were the Israelites successful in conquering the land, but they were acting as one community, all embracing God's plan. There was none of the grumbling or complaining that was rampant in the wilderness. And it's not that the Israelites are stuffing down any resistance; God and the Israelites under Joshua are simply moving as one unit, one community.

---

[203] Gerald G. May, *The Dark Night of the Soul,* Harper One, New York, 2004, p. 75

[204] Ibid, pp. 77-8

[205] Thomas Merton, *New Seeds of Contemplation,* A New Directions Book, New York, 1961, p. 283

Joshua represents that part of us who can commune with God, answer to Him, obey Him and worship Him. He represents the heart and the mind moving in concert. He draws his courage and trust and strength from the Lord. And so, he is the archetype of the leader needed on the last part of the journey with Christ where we move in tandem with Him, where we are co-partnering with God, accomplishing all that God has set as the goal for us. He watches out for all challenges to God's sovereignty. He leads us into battle over the world's ways that are deep in our unconscious, those entrenched interests in various parts of our psyche. He is courageous, because he is so connected to God. He roots out the rebelliousness (as in Achan's sin) and leads us into battle with the powers that be, successfully, because he is so attuned to God. He does his work in God for the good of the whole community.

And that fulfills another of the aspects of union with God: community. We have entered a community, the Kingdom, the covenant with God where everyone's willingness to say "Yes!" to God is equal, where everyone has but one desire, to serve God. William Clemmons writes: "Community is that place where we enter into the presence of each other and the Lord who called us there, as fully and totally as we do in the engagements with ourselves and God. It is a place that calls us to abandon ourselves to each other, for in so doing, we discover ourselves. It is a place where we are available to each other as we have learned to be with God. It is a place where we are totally present to each other, aware of each other, and are listening to each other with the totality of our being. It is a coming together because Christ has called us to be committed to Him and to each other through His gift of *koinonia*."[206]

I want to cite the lives of three late 19th and 20th century men to illustrate how someone in union with God operates in the challenges of the world: missionary John G. Paton, theologian, and pastor Dietrich Bonhoeffer and Fr. Walter Ciszek. In very different, but equally threatening and challenging situations, these three men worked without fear of anything, totally trusting in God, each in their own way.

John G. Paton was a Scottish missionary at the end of the 19th century to the New Hebrides, a group of islands off the east coast of Australia. Each island had multiple tribes of cannibals that were totally at war with one another. Paton was a missionary to two of the islands over forty years of time. He stood up to armed villagers wanting to kill him and eat him many times; he was only armed with God's love, which he communicated to them over and over again. He endured personal losses--one wife and two children. Over the forty years he spent in the Hebrides late in the 19th century and early 20th, he and other missionaries converted the islands to Christianity, to living peacefully, faithfully together in a place that had been completely savage. I have a picture of him in my mind standing tall among the native populations armed and hostile and himself totally at peace. His autobiography, *John G. Paton, Missionary to the New Hebrides: An Autobiography,* is a fascinating read.

---

[206] William Clemmons, *Discovering the Depths: Guidance in Spiritual Growth,* Triangle Publishing, London, 1987, p.88, koinonia has the connotation in Greek of community and communion.

From a missionary, we now turn to German theologian and pastor, Dietrich Bonhoeffer who was executed by the Nazis just at the end of World War II. He had been imprisoned for his active and vocal opposition to the Nazi regime, particularly to the Nazi's taking over the German Lutheran Church and imposing its standards on the Biblical religion. He objected to the treatment of the Jews. And was a key member and founder of the Confessing Church, which stood for the Biblical tradition and values in opposition to the Reichskirche, the official Nazi "church."

Bonhoeffer was a visionary, a prophet from the time that the Nazis first came to power in Germany in the early 30's. He had grown up in a family that was quite prominent and privileged in Berlin. His father's side of the family were scientists; his mother's theologians. By the age of thirteen he had declared that he wanted to be a theologian. In the early 1930's, in his mid-20's, he was teaching theology in Berlin. He recognized from the beginning of the Nazis' rise to power the disastrous turn that Germany was about to take. He spent a year in New York City mainly influenced by worship in African-American churches. He spent time in Spain and in London serving German congregations. So he was able to identify with a broader identity than that of a German Christian.

As the Nazi's gained power and exercised it over the Jews and dissidents and disabled, they established the Reichskircke and rewrote the Gospel to their liking and threw out the Old Testament. Bonhoeffer was a key player in resisting the Nazi influence in the Church and in establishing the Confessing Church as the only Christian church in Germany. In all his activities he was way ahead of his time; others in the church were more forgiving of the Nazi penetration until it was too late. In 1937 he published his book, *The Cost of Discipleship,* which is considered a classic. Bonhoeffer also ran an underground seminary "on the run" as he dodged the Gestapo, which shut it down in 1940. By 1941 he was forbidden to print or publish. He joined the Abwehr, the German military intelligence organization.

Under their auspices he traveled to Norway, Sweden and Switzerland and connected with the broader ecumenical church, helped German Jews escape to Switzerland and was finally arrested in April 1943. From prison he wrote *Letters and Papers from Prison.* Later he was transferred to Flossenburg concentration camp where he was executed on April 8, 1945, just at the end of the European war. He is remembered today for his passionate defense of the Church, of Jesus' teachings and of his willingness to stand up to evil, even at the cost of his own life.

The third life I want to highlight is that of Fr. Walter Ciszek, an Ignatian priest newly ordained and in Poland at the beginning of World War II. He was a Polish-American man who had been active in gangs before he shocked his family by becoming a priest. He studied theology and the Russian language in Rome from 1934 to 1937. From there he went to eastern Poland where in 1941, he was arrested by the Russians for "spying for the Vatican."

He spent four years in solitary confinement and being tortured in the infamous Lubyanka Prison in Moscow, then fifteen years at hard labor in Siberia. He had to remain in Siberia after his release until he was swapped for a Russian prisoner and able to return to the United States. While at hard labor, he managed secretly to serve communion to his fellow prisoners and worked very hard at the hard work he was given, because he felt that he was still and always working for God. In the several years he had to remain "free" in Russia, he established secret mission parishes for the locals. Here is a quote that captures his attitude during these long years:

"Across that threshold I had been afraid to cross, things suddenly seemed so very simple. There was but a single vision, God, who was all in all; there was but one will that directed all things, God's will. I had only to see it, to discern it in every circumstance in which I found myself, and let myself be ruled by it. God is in all things, sustains all things, directs all things. To discern this in every situation and circumstance, to see His will in all things, was to accept each circumstance and situation and let oneself be borne along in perfect confidence and trust. Nothing could separate me from Him, because He was in all things. No danger could threaten me, no fear could shake me, except the fear of losing sight of Him. The future, hidden as it was, was hidden in His will and therefore acceptable to me no matter what it might bring.

"The past, with all its failures, was not forgotten; it remained to remind me of the weakness of human nature and the folly of putting any faith in self. But it no longer depressed me. I looked no longer to self to guide me, relied on it no longer in any way, so it could not again fail me. By renouncing, finally and completely, all control of my life and future destiny, I was relieved as a consequence of all responsibility. I was freed thereby from anxiety and worry, from every tension, and could float serenely upon the tide of God's sustaining providence in perfect peace of soul."[207]

In a state of union with God there is abundant courage, faith, everything one needs to sustain life. And then there is the impact that a person in union with God has on the fellow-prisoners in Bonhoeffer's and Ciszek's stories and on the native cannibals in Paton's. This is love in its highest form in a human being, faith to the utmost and God's faithfulness all revealed in these courageous acts.

Seamless co-participation with God, living and working in the community of the Kingdom of God, where the fruit of the Spirit[208] reign—these are the realizations of those living in the Promised Land. And I do mean realizations. Each of us has the capacity to live in the Promised Land, to love God with all of ourselves, to complete these four stages of the spiritual journey. Whether that capacity is ever brought forward in our lives and consumes all our attachments to the ways of the world is a question for each of us together with God to answer. But we have the God-given capacity built into us.

The Promised Land, the Kingdom of God, is not a place with property and a home for each person. It is a state of consciousness, a joint state of consciousness with God and everyone else, in which we are totally at home in ourselves, where all our needs are provided, where God is the center of

---

[207] www.goodreads.com/author/quotes/398414.Walter_J_Ciszek
[208] "love, joy, peace, forbearance, kindness, goodness, faithfulness, gentleness and self-control"Galatians 5:22-23

everything, and where the community is everything. It is what Paul called "hav[ing] the mind of Christ."[209]

Detachment from the world

With every tribe conquered, with every city either destroyed or invaded and captured, Canaan becomes the symbol of the disintegration of everything human that lives in our psyches. For the Israelites it was the outer landscape that held so many challenges, peoples to conquer, armies to defeat. For us it is an inner territory full of perils and pain and suffering. But, as we are co-participants with God, we will follow God's leadings and methods, we will succeed and thrive in this new "land." All the human tendencies to power, represented by the 31 kings who were killed by Joshua and the Israelites--[210]have to go, as we nestle deeper and deeper into the mind of Christ and God with the Holy Spirit. Many of the peoples, their kings, their possessions and especially their sacred things have to be destroyed. They will have no purchase in us in the Promised Land. In the Kingdom, all that matters is of God.

Not every conquered people are destroyed. And so, even in the Kingdom, we live among those who do not follow God, who would tempt us to live their ways and worship their gods. As long as we live on this Earth, we are awash in the temptations of the world. We need to keep vigilant about following God in order to live in this Promised Land. As the history of the Israelites reveals, in the time of the Judges, the Israelites' covenant with God breaks down and the whole community comes to no longer even

---

[209] 1 Corinthians 2:16
[210] Joshua 12:9-24 This passage lists all 31 kings.

caring to serve God. But that is a story beyond the scope of this book.

In this Exodus story there came a time when the Israelites settled into their new homes in the new land. There is still more land to conquer, but they settle into their own communities; they tend their own crops and animals; they enjoy the fruit of all their labors and rest from fighting the hostile peoples and their kings and gods. They live out their purposes; they live in community with each other. They are blessed by the very land in which they live.

And so it is with us in the Kingdom of God. We pursue our purposes with God's help. We relax into the freedom of God's sovereignty. We've shed all the burdens of our past and are free to be who we were created to be and to totally follow the Lord's lead.

Even in the Promised Land the people will need to be vigilant in following God's laws, just as we will need the same vigilance in rooting out any rebellion within us. The entrenched interests about to be conquered in this new land are the attachments of a lifetime within us as well as whatever parts of our human nature would separate us from God—which we must conquer, with God's help, one at a time. As we face each kingdom to which we have given over our power in the past, we need to "conquer," to let go of their influence over our true home. As always, we do that with God's help. It is a last look for us at the power of our own attachments, but now easy to release, because their power over us is gone as each of us, too, becomes the servant of the Lord.

Rebellion

Achan represents the last of the ego-centered impulses in us. Any chance of us following those urges will lead us to defeat God's agenda for us. And we, if we follow any of these urges, will die to them. Where once God allowed us that choice in the wilderness, now that option is gone. Our bad choices will wipe us out, bring on the worse of the curses that God detailed in Deuteronomy28.[211] Once we cross the Jordan River, once we live in the Kingdom of God, once we are filled with the Holy Spirit, there is no room for rebellion. The only choice is to die to our former life.

Each intransient power within us that has not been purged in the wilderness—read the 31 kings whom the Israeli's defeated—has to go. All the errant power within us. All that is unconscious that would take us away from God's ways.

While this may seem harsh, it is the reality of the Kingdom. Anything that diverts us from God's agenda for us has to go. Everything in the Kingdom points to Life in its fullest sense, to Love in its greatest application, to embracing others in all that they are, to being a true community where everyone belongs and is equal, no matter their gifts and talents. The only one who stands above anyone else in the Kingdom is Christ Himself. There is no hierarchy in the Kingdom.[212]

---

[211] vs. 15-68

[212] For a full description of the Kingdom of God, I refer you to my book, *Thy Kingdom Come*, Amazon.com, 2015.

Even the Gibeonites who tried to trick the Israelites into a treaty found themselves servants to the Israelites in Canaan when the truth emerged. No rebellion, no lies allowed.

As rebellion is quelled in the kingdom, the rebels are either destroyed or come to serve the Lord. Some are allowed to live. The stories in the Book of Joshua are of the Israelites led by Joshua conquering nations, destroying some peoples and some cities, destroying any devotional items, sometimes destroying, sometimes taking over the herds. Everything comes under the aegis of the Lord our God.

The Covenant

I had an epiphany while doing the research on Part IV of this book, on union with God, that thrilled me. It was this: the Covenant which God gave to Abraham and reaffirmed many times in the Old Testament, which He reaffirmed with the Israelites in the Exodus story several times is a covenant with the whole tribe of Israel.[213] I had always just thought about my relationship with God or another person's, not with the whole people. And that thought just blew me away!

I have long thought that the Kingdom was a true community where everyone not only belonged, in which everyone was honored for whatever contribution s/he made,[214] but I now believe that the Covenant that we "sign" with God for being His people as we are "born-again" or surrender our lives to God and devote our own selves 100%

---

[213] Exodus 2:24, 6:4, 5, 19:5, 24:7, for example. There are many references in all 5 books of the Exodus story—Exodus, Leviticus, Numbers, Deuteronomy and Joshua.
[214] Patricia Said Adams, *Thy Kingdom Come!*, Amazon, pp. 94-97

to God, includes all of us, all people no matter whether they follow God or not. But for those of us in union with God, who live in the Kingdom of God, we are to embrace the whole world of people as being part of our covenant with God: to love, to be at peace with, to take joy in, to have patience with, to be good and kind to, to be faithful to, to be gentle with and to have self-control so that we can set aside our own needs (knowing that God will fill them always) in order to serve the one(s) before me.[215]

Everyone belongs to our community in God whether they have committed themselves to Him or whether they live in the "real" world or not. They are our people and we are to treat them accordingly. The Covenant with Abraham and Isaac and Jacob and so on is our covenant, too. I do not want to take anything from the Israelites and the Jews; they still remain God's Chosen People. They have been the test case for all humanity, the proof that we can serve the Lord our God. But the onus for the Kingdom of God is on all of us now. We are all called to promote the Kingdom and to preserve all life in doing that.

Conquering the Territory

What characterized Canaan so well was its people's worship of other gods and their fear of the God of Abraham and Isaac. Although these are primitive peoples were without our common wireless communication, nevertheless the word spread quickly throughout the land of the power and might of the armies of Israel and their God, even before they arrived at the River Jordan. Resistance arose in different ways. Achan, an Israelite, rebelled by ignoring God's laws.

---

[215] Galatians 5:22-3 The fruit of the Spirit

The Gibeonites try to deceive Joshua and the Israelites into not attacking them by lying about where they are from. They have to become servants of Israel. Thirty-one kings are killed, their kingdoms destroyed, either one-by-one or as they banded together. They were right to fear the Lord; He defeated them all. Thirty-one is a large number of largely unconscious power centers within our unconscious which would lead us away from God. So, as we live in the Promised Land, we have to tackle them one-by-one or in groups to destroy their power over us, so that we, in the end, have only one loyalty to, one covenant with God.

And still, years after we entered Canaan, there is still territory to conquer, kings' armies to conquer. Maybe within us humans there is an endless spate of rebellion just waiting to happen. At least that, to me, is what the Exodus story suggests: That there is no end to the power struggles within us or outside of us. But all we have to do until the day we die is follow God's lead and we will not violate our own covenant with Him-- ever.

Rituals

As we enter the Kingdom of God, we are asked to follow the Ark of the Covenant which houses the laws of God. That is to be the symbol of our fidelity to the letter of the law and the spirit of the law. The waters of the River Jordan are being held back just as those of the Red Sea were forty years before, so that in walking into the river we might be descended upon by the Holy Spirit, henceforth led solely by Him. We pick a stone out of the riverbed to commemorate this personal "Pentecost." Our hearts[216] are

---

[216] Deuteronomy 10:16

circumcised to symbolize our adherence to God's Covenant with His people going all the way back to Abraham, so that our bodies, souls and our hearts and spirit would carry out God's laws.[217] Then we are to celebrate "Passover," to remember always what God has done in our lives. It's the end of our journey all the way from Egypt, from slavery to the world; it's our arrival in the Kingdom of God, now that we are setting foot in Canaan.

The renewal of the Covenant with God is such a common occurrence in the Exodus story. It behooves us to do that regularly, too. It could be a monthly or yearly practice wherein we affirm our covenant with God for our lives and our commitment to follow it faithfully. God certainly doesn't need the reminder, but He may appreciate our recommitment on a regular basis.

At each milestone along the way the Israelites erect piles of stones to commemorate—the crossing of the Jordan, honoring the loving support and care of their God. And so, we, too, are to remember all that God has done for us.

Distribution of the land

At long last after killing off thirty-one kings and conquering their territory, land and people, lands are assigned to each tribe. What I find amazing is that there is no squabbling over who gets which land. Even with the casting of lots for the last seven tribes, there is little envy. After all the wars the people are ready to settle, and, I project, grateful to have a home of their own. And so it is with us in the Kingdom. We are given a place that is ours, a purpose

---

[217] http://www.biblestudytools.com/dictionary/circumcision/

that is unique. There is no competition because each allotment is based on our own talents and gifts and even challenges. We are all equally needed there. We are beyond comparing, beyond feeling less-than someone else, way beyond the egocentricity and the complaints that were so strikingly obvious in the purgation period.

We are at peace and so is everyone else in the Kingdom. There will always be challenges (read other nations in the Exodus story); I believe, at least in this lifetime, but with God leading us, we will always be up to the challenge. That promise we can trust, because we have the experience of God keeping His promises time and again in our lives and in this Old Testament story. Some of the peoples we have conquered will be among us, within us, but all we have to do is to keep our eyes on God and not to follow their practices, their gods.

Kingdom of God

In my book, *Thy Kingdom Come!*, I likened the Kingdom of God to the agora, an ancient Greek marketplace where everyone gathered every day for news, for support, for community. But "unlike the *agora*, the Kingdom is not a place; it is a state of heart and mind. It is a home for those of us who are in this world, but not of the world. It is not a place for perfect people only for those who would bring their whole selves to God in love. It is the wheat among the tares until the harvest, coexisting like a parallel universe right next to what we consider the 'real world.' Those who carry the Kingdom in their hearts and minds bring it with them, wherever they go. There is challenge and even suffering, but no one is ever alone: God is walking through life with us every step of the way, and then we have these companions, others who now live in the Kingdom, along the way."[218]

In the Exodus story Canaan, the Promised Land, represents the Kingdom of God, of heaven, the culmination of the spiritual journey on Earth. It is a state of mind, not a literal place. It is where our minds are joined in Christ's mind, where we are totally aligned in God's will, where everywhere we go we bring evidence of the Kingdom—the fruit of the Spirit—peace, joy, love, patience, goodness, kindness, faithfulness, gentleness and self-control—to pour out of ourselves, giving back to the world. All challenges are easily overcome, because we are absolutely following the will of God. Total trust in God, total dependence on God and total freedom to be who we were created to be are the watchwords of the Kingdom. No one holds back anything. Everyone is filled with the Spirit of God, which now replaces the ego, the ways of the world superseded by God's ways, and with His Spirit.

The Kingdom had been promised to the Israelites since God called Abraham,[219] but it has taken this long to be realized, because the human beings, the Israelites had to be transformed to be able to live there. They had to go through the three stages of the spiritual journey—*awakening, purgation and illumination*—before they would be filled with the Holy Spirit and enter the Kingdom in that state of purity and holiness, into *union* with God. As I wrote earlier in the book, Abraham was the first to live in the Kingdom—witness his willing sacrifice of Isaac, his son. He was totally

---

[218] Patricia Said Adams, *Thy Kingdom Come!*, Amazon, 2015, p. 96-7
[219] Genesis 22:1-19

willing to give God exactly what He asked, without reservation. And it was through his progeny that later Israelites were able to enter into that same state of willingness and love of God.

Part IV: The Promised Land

Chapter Three

Lessons from the Book of Joshua

The Kingdom is the place where love reigns, where God's love permeates everything and everyone. It is the place where we are total partners of God, moving and stopping at His direction, heeding all His suggestions. It is the place where each of us is equally welcome, equally important in spreading the word about the Kingdom of God. And it exists here on Earth, if we will only love God with all of ourselves. Jesus describes the Kingdom as around, within and here,[220] as if all we need to do is to discover it, claim our interest in a deep relationship with God, and come to live in it. If we're no longer rebellious about anything, then we will follow God wherever He leads.

Our human lives are marked by yearnings, often very subtle yearnings for peace, for fulfillment, for God. What we

---

[220] Matthew 10:7, Mark 1:15, Luke 10:9, 17:21, 21:31

don't, for the most part, realize is that the more we rest in God's arms, follow what He offers us and discover our purpose in this life and live it, the more we will find fulfillment, contentment, peace and ease. To all the questions and yearning in our lives, there is but one answer: God. All our longings cannot be filled by more and more material stuff. The perfect job will not suffice, nor will a beautiful wife or husband, not even enough money. That is all that the culture offers us for fulfillment. If you've tried to find fulfillment through any or all of these paths, you have been left with longing for something more and have been greatly disappointed.

There is only one answer to all the dilemmas we encounter in this life: God. God in our marriage; God in our work; God in our leisure; God in our parenting. God everywhere in our lives is the answer. And in some ways that does not mean religion. It just means that we partner with God, we defer to Wisdom Himself; we follow His suggestions for what to do and how to do it. He is our constant companion and mentor on this road to fulfillment. No one else can tell you what God intends for you, but God. Others can share pointers, but each of us must take responsibility for the relationship by deepening and deepening our ties to God Himself and not depending on a single other person to define and delineate what we are to do. God is to be our sole source of wisdom--both from the Bible and from His Indwelling Spirit.

Then, where does religion fit in, you might ask? Religion reinforces our beliefs, gives us a place to worship God, helps keep us on track, provides companions along the way, a real community, a place to pursue our purpose, but it is no substitute for the personal relationship with God.

Our own inner Joshua arises as our inner interface with God in the midst of the purgation stage. He is our companion and exemplar of the two later stages of the spiritual journey: *Illumination* and *Union*. It is His integrity and leadership, His warrior's mentality that will take us across the Jordan River into Canaan. Moses came from our very humanness, a flawed human being who was nonetheless able to hear God speak and to almost always follow God's instructions. Joshua has never rebelled at all.

Joshua, at the end of his life, spoke to the Israelites his farewell. "Be very strong; be careful to obey all that is written in the Book of the Law of Moses, without turning aside to the right or to the left. Do not associate with these nations that remain among you; do not invoke the names of their gods or swear by them. You must not serve them or bow down to them. But you are to hold fast to the Lord your God, as you have until now."[221] And then he reiterates the blessings and curses of Deuteronomy, reminding them of the built-in rewards of following the Law and the punishment of disobedience.[222]

He is reminding the Israelites to keep God at the forefront of their lives, to follow where He leads, to not rebel, to ignore the Law. Above all, he is saying that following God and His law is to live fully, and to love fully. These are also lessons for us.

---

[221] Joshua 23:6-8
[222] Joshua 23:15-16

Joshua teaches us how we are to be with God through two *inclusios,* as theologian Dr. John D. Currid suggests. An *inclusio*is a literary device, a way of bracketing, used by Biblical writers that provides emphasis in a passage or in this case, a book of the Bible. By bracketing a story or the Book of Joshua, for example, with a repeating theme, the writer is underlining certain aspects of the story.

The first *inclusio* in the Book of Joshua is that Moses was called "the servant of the Lord" in Joshua 1:1. And at the end of Joshua in Chapter 24:9, Joshua was likewise titled, "the servant of the Lord."[223] Here the author of Joshua is underscoring Joshua's importance to the story; he was the equal of Moses, equally faithful and true to the Lord. For us, to be called the servant of the Lord means that we have been a faithful follower of all the Lord has said to us. It is high praise, indeed.

The second *inclusio* comes in Joshua 1 as God speaks to Joshua after the death of Moses: "Be strong and very courageous. Be careful to obey all the law my servant Moses gave you; do not turn from it to the right or to the left, that you may be successful wherever you go. Keep this Book of the Law always on your lips; meditate on it day and night, so that you may be careful to do everything written in it. Then you will be prosperous and successful. Have I not commanded you? Be strong and courageous. Do not be afraid; do not be discouraged, for the Lord your God will be with you wherever you go."[224]

[223] John D. Currid, *Strong and Courageous: Joshua simply Explained,* EP Books, Carlisle PA, 2011, p. 259
[224] Joshua 1:7-9

Hear Joshua now at the end of his life echoing the same teaching as he says farewell to the Israelites at the end of the Book of Joshua: "Be very strong; be careful to obey all that is written in the Book of the Law of Moses, without turning aside to the right or to the left. Do not associate with these nations that remain among you; do not invoke the names of their gods or swear by them. You must not serve them or bow down to them. But you are to hold fast to the Lord your God, as you have until now."[225]

Hold fast to the Lord your God. Trust in God. Remain faithful. Do not deviate from the Commandments. Be so caught up in loving God that you cannot break any of the Commands that He holds dear. If we hold to the first four of the Ten Commandments, we cannot break any of the others, because of our love for God. The repetition in the *inclusio* here just emphasizes what God has said all along in His Covenant with Abraham and his descendants: "I will remember the covenant with their ancestors whom I brought out of Egypt in the sight of the nations to be their God. I am the Lord."[226] Our part of the Covenant is to obedient and to follow Him.

---

[225] Joshua 23:6-8
[226] Leviticus 26:45

Part V

CONCLUSIONS

The Exodus of the Israelites from Egypt through the long journey in the wilderness to settling in Canaan or the Promised Land is the template that God has left us in the Exodus story. There are four stages to this process of conversion from slavery to the world to God's Kingdom: *Awakening, Purgation, Illumination, Union*—these are the stages of the spiritual journey when undertaken by a person who seriously desires a deeper and deeper relationship with God.

In order to travel this way we have to have some sort of *awakening* experience in which we see that whatever the world is offering pales in comparison to the full, rich and fulfilling life that God invites us to live with Him. It may be that we finally tire of the endless accumulation of more and more stuff that never fulfills. We might be thrown out of the world by an illness or a close friend's or a family member's death. It might be a job loss that makes us wake up to new possibilities. We might be real tired of the treadmill we are on. Or we might just answer one of the endless invitations God sends us to come to Him, because we are longing for more.

However it is that we get dislodged from the world's influence doesn't matter. What is important is that we wake up and see a whole new possibility for us, a way that is more integral to who we are, that will affirm and challenge and support us in going down a whole new road which is never offered by the world.

Our decision to leave the world's cares behind and to focus on God's will brings us to the wilderness where the issues that block us from God will be highlighted and healed and where whatever is problematic in us as humans, will be transformed. The wilderness is a place where we will be tested by the lack of everything, by the tastelessness of the food (nourishment), the difficulty finding water (which cleanses and washes away all unnecessary stuff), the unfamiliarity of the landscape and its harshness, the vulnerability that we feel, and the uncertainty that exists in every moment of every day. In the wilderness, God is clearly in charge and we are never quite certain that what is happening is good for us. He is more present to us, more visible, but this is not always comforting, for we have to give up our own ways of dealing with all this vulnerability and uncertainty in favor of God's ways. We have to move from our attachment to the past to living in the present with God.

This period of *purgation*, of cleansing, of healing and eventually of transformation could not happen in our ordinary lives unless we have already found ourselves in the wilderness—there are far too many distractions there for us to totally focus on what God is saying to us and where He is leading us. Certainly, we are most often still living those normal lives of family and work and leisure, as we feel ourselves thrown into the wilderness. Only a natural disaster or losing our homes, something that takes us out of the "normal" lives that we lead, wrenches us away from that normal stuff without some notice that we are leaving the world (Egypt) and all its influence.

Essentially what we have to give up is our free will, our expectations, our assumptions about life and how it should go, and our way of tackling life. We have to give up our rebellious ways and surrender everything, that is *EVERYTHING*, in us to God! The big things and the small stuff. Often it is our objection to whatever is happening to us today, right now, that we must surrender. We must come to the conclusion that we can trust God in everything to do what is exactly right for us in every instance. We have to give up our objections to how our lives go and capitulate to Him at every turn. We must lay down our arms and stop the good fight, give up our rebelliousness and with wide-open arms, welcome what God is sending us or allow it to come into our lives! That's all, but we must let go of every single thing that keeps us from bringing our whole selves before God in love.

Our conversion is not something that happens in us at the moment we commit our lives to God. It took the Israelites forty years before they were finally purged of all their rebellions and were actually ready to follow wherever God was going to lead them. The old generation had to die off, if not literally at least figuratively, the old way of thinking and being had to die. It was forty years of learning to trust that God would keep His promises, that He would take care of them, not just with manna and water and quail, but fulfilling every need they might have. Trust in God, obedience to His will for us, a willingness, an openness to do whatever He suggests, and finally an ability to see as God sees—these are the qualities we need to move into the *illumination* stage of the spiritual journey. In this stage we are very close to God, partnering with Him and yet, still in the world. It takes a long time for these qualities of total surrender to develop in us.

For our part we can offer our lives to God, we can make the commitment steadfast by our willing pursuit of any way that we don't conform to His ways, but we cannot do the healing work or the transformative work that will bring us to the person God created us to be. Only God can do that. Only God can unite our lives with His. *Union* is the ultimate and last stage. It used to be considered that we achieved perfection if we were very good and died and went to heaven. There we were united with God. But Jesus taught that the Kingdom is here and now, around and among and within us. It is a potential within all human beings to live in the Kingdom on this Earth.[227]

God is consistently, throughout our lives, planting seeds of invitation for us to give up our worldly ways, to live deeper into our own lives and to live in His Kingdom. He invites us to surrender all that we have taken on since our birth and return to the very being that He created us to be, to live in His arms, to co-partner our lives with Him. All we have to do is say, "Yes!" and He will show us everything we will need to know. It's clear in the Exodus story that He meets all their needs—physical (food and water and camps),

---

[227] Matthew 3:2, Luke 17:21

mental (standards of living to ponder and to adopt) and spiritual (connected to Him as He is always visible) and heart felt (through an individual relationship with God and through a close community).

Following God is not the easy way we might envision. Leaving home and giving up our way of doing everything is full of challenges, of loss, of vulnerability and pain. Many times the Israelites longed to go back to the life of slavery which in the wilderness began to take on the aura of a perfect life, not at all like the discomfort of living in the wilderness! And so do we long for what used to be. But the journey is self-affirming, affirming of our deepest self and of a deepening relationship with God which does begin to draw us away from our pre-occupation with all the world's ways and how we like to live and be in the world. We begin to see the bigger picture of life as God sees it. We begin to live into that larger picture of what life and love are all about.

We begin to see, with God's help, where and how He is calling us to spend our lives, to see our calling, our purpose and how to fulfill it. He knows us so well—our gifts and talents and even challenges that He created in us and how to use them for the glory of His Kingdom. Whether those talents are of woodworking or weaving or speaking or whatever; our talents are intended to be used for the realization of the Kingdom on this Earth. What is so interesting to me is how He uses our challenges, once healed and transformed. Often we are to serve the people with the same challenges that we have faced and overcome—ex-alcoholic to alcoholics, or a cancer-survivor to other cancer-survivors, abuse sufferers to other abuse sufferers, ex-cons to prisoners or other ex-cons, for example.

The "wounded healer" speaks the same language, understands the challenges of the condition others and the lies we tell ourselves so we don't have to change. We tend to listen to people who know our condition because they have lived it. Everyone else trying to help an alcoholic, say, or other addict, is just preaching without intimate knowledge of what they are talking about.

In the Exodus template, God is showing us how to be with Him. He is holding out hope and integrity and love and forgiveness for us so that we might come into our own as our own true selves, living not from the world's perspective, but from God's. We are to grow into our innate capacity to love and to forgive as God loves and forgives, to have integrity where what people see in us is our own internal conditions as well, to be able to treat everyone as anyone would like to be treated, to utilize all that we are in service to God. And so we fulfill the destiny that God designed in us, in His arms, with His methods, using all that we are.

The benefits of moving along the whole arc of the Exodus story and template are legion: freedom and more freedom to be as we were created to be, comfort and support and mentoring all along the way, a purposeful life contributing to the growth and visibility of the Kingdom of God, and the acquiring of the fruit of the Spirit, the ability to love as described in Galatians 5:23-24: in peace, joy, patience, goodness, kindness, faithfulness, gentleness and self-control. Living in the Kingdom of God means that we are living life to the fullest, obedient to God in the freest way possible, and surrounded by love, and forgiveness, blessings and grace. What's not to love about that?

In so many ways the Exodus story is the story of who our God is. He keeps His covenants and His promises. Occasionally, He gets angry at the Israelites and He seems swift in punishing any rebellion—all the rebels in the story die immediately with the exception of the whole generation of Israelites whom He rescued from Egypt. After so much grumbling and worshipping another god, He swears that they will not enter the Promised Land. They will die in the desert.

I think that we have to be careful not to assign too much importance to these displays of anger or to project that God is an angry God with a thunderbolt in the sky, just waiting for a chance to punish us. First, God is very clear about our part in His world, His Kingdom. We are to obey His law and commandments. The Israelites grumbled and complained about everything once they crossed the Red Sea. Their acts of rebellion have included this complaining as well as direct disobedience in building a golden calf to worship and sexual immorality with the Moabite women who enticed them to eat sacrificial meats for their gods and then to bow down to them. God was not only angry, but deeply disappointed that they strayed so far after being rescued from slavery. But He is slow to anger.[228]

Secondly, I think the deaths are more symbolic than actual. The men and women who rebelled against God represent our own human nature. In big ways and small, some of our greatest challenges in trying to lead a spiritual

---

[228] Exodus 34:6

life in God are our awareness [or not] of where we stray and our willingness to address our sin in ourselves. It is far easier to see sin in another than in ourselves, but still the rebellion in us has to die.

Thirdly, God did not get so angry that He threatened to wipe out the whole Israelite community. He targeted specific behavior, not everyone He could see. Unlike any human tyrant, God reserves His anger for those who deserve it. And we have to balance any picture of God's anger with his keeping His promises to the Israelites and His obvious love for them.

Fourth, God is bound by His covenant with the Israelites. It only takes a small reminder from Moses about the covenant to get Him to back off His anger.[229]

And the story is about us human beings, too. The Israelites represent all human beings in this story, in this template about the life God calls us to. Given free will, we have a rebellious, fractious nature. We like things the way we like them. Even when we have given our lives over to God, it takes a long time to address our own rebellion and to fully align our wills with God's will. This template for moving from a world-centered will to embracing God's will for us takes a long time to accomplish. We accomplish little of this on our own; our part is to be faithful as we can to God, to persevere no matter what, and to bring our whole selves, warts and all, before God in love.[230]

---

[229] Exodus 32:9-14
[230] Jesus' Two Great Commandments Matthew 22:36-40, Mark 12:28-31, Luke 10:25-27

Then it is up to God to heal and transform our pain and suffering and rebelliousness into God-willing people. In the process of all this healing the ego comes under the aegis of the soul, and the rebellion goes. Mostly, we are letting go of our world-centered, culture-centered selves in favor of the true self, which would nestle in God arms. We move from the influence of the past and worries about the future into the present where we find God always.

Bibliography

Benedict J. Groeschel, *Spiritual Passages: The Psychology of Spiritual Development,* The Crossroad Publishing Company, New York, 1983.

Chris Webb, *The Fire of the Word: Meeting God on Holy Ground,* IVP Books, Downers Grove IL, 2011.

Edward W. Goodrick& John R. Kohlenberger III, *Zondervan NIV Exhaustive Concordance, 2nd Edition,* Zondervan Publishing House, Grand Rapids, MI, 1999.

Evelyn Underhill, *Mysticism: A Study in the Nature and Development of Spiritual Consciousness,* Dover Publications, Inc., Mineola NY, 2002.

Gerald G. May, M.D., *The Dark Night of the Soul: A Psychiatrist Explores the Connection Between Darkness and Spiritual Growth,* Harper One, New York, 2004.
Jean-Pierre de Caussade, *The Sacrament of the Present Moment,* translator by William Collins Sons & Co., HarperOne, New York, 1981.

John D. Currid, *Strong and Courageous: Joshua simply Explained,* EP Books, Carlisle PA, 2011.

M. Robert Mulholland, Jr., *Invitation to a Journey: A Road Map for Spiritual Formation,* IVP Books, Downers Grove IL, 1993.

Patricia Said Adams, *Thy Kingdom Come!* Amazon.com, 2015.

Richard J. Foster, *Prayer: Finding the Heart's True Home,* Harper Large Print Edition, New York, 1992.

Sue Monk Kidd, *When the Heart Waits: Spiritual Direction for Life's Sacred Questions,* Harper One, New York, 1990.

Thomas Merton, *New Seeds of Contemplation,* A New Directions Book, New York, 1961.

William Clemmons, *Discovering the Depths: Guidance in Spiritual Growth,* Broadman Press, London, 1987.

ABOUT THE AUTHOR

Patricia Said Adams, known as Pat, was born in 1941; she spent most of her childhood in Louisville, Kentucky, and her teens in Wilmington, Delaware. She graduated from Connecticut College in 1963 with a BA in Art History. She has worked in banking and retailing; her favorite job was as a women's sportswear buyer. She and her husband raised three children; he supported the family and she was a school and church volunteer.

She has been a Spiritual Director for 15 years, a supervisor of spiritual directors for six years and a blogger about the spiritual life for nine years. She so enjoys the privilege of working with others at the soul level. The central question of her life is this: how do I, how do we, live the life God intends for us?

Thy Kingdom Come! is her first book AND her second book is, *Exodus: Our Story Too! From Slavery to the World to the Kingdom of God.*

CONTACT PATRICIA SAID ADAMS AT:

Exodus: Our Story Too! – http://exodus-our-story-too.blogspot.com

Patricia Said Adams - http://patricia-said-adams.blogspot.com

By The Waters Blog – http://bythewaters.net

52732462R00133

Made in the USA
San Bernardino, CA
28 August 2017